CYCLIN
SOUTH
AND W

GREAT ROAD ROUTES

IAN O'RIORDAN has been a sports reporter with *The Irish Times* since 1998. He was born in Dublin, ran for Ireland as a junior, and spent four years on a running scholarship in America. He has run several marathons, including Athens, New York and Honolulu. He first took to road cycling in 2006 and has since ridden several major road routes throughout Europe, including the famous Alpine stages from Geneva to Nice. He lives in Glencullen, on the Dublin/Wicklow Mountains border.

@ianoriordan

Cycling is a risk sport. The author and The Collins Press accept no responsibility for any injury, loss or inconvenience sustained by anyone using this guidebook.

To reduce the chance of break-in to parked cars, cyclists are advised to place all valuables and belongings out of sight.

Advice to Readers

Every effort is made by our authors to ensure the accuracy of our guidebooks. However, changes can occur after a book has been printed, including changes to rights of way. If you notice discrepancies between this guidebook and the facts on the ground, please let us know, either by email to enquiries@collinspress.ie or by post to The Collins Press, West Link Park, Doughcloyne, Wilton, Cork, T12 N5EF, Ireland.

Looking out over the Cloghoge Valley at Luggala

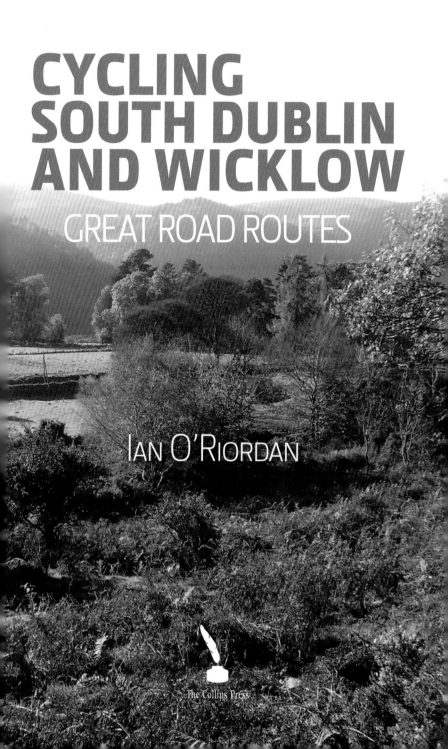

CYCLING
SOUTH DUBLIN
AND WICKLOW

GREAT ROAD ROUTES

Ian O'Riordan

The Collins Press

First published in 2018 by
The Collins Press
West Link Park
Doughcloyne
Wilton
Cork
T12 N5EF
Ireland

A CIP record for this book is available from the British Library.

Paperback ISBN: 978-1-84889-344-3

Design and typesetting by Fairways Design
Typeset in Myriad Pro
Printed in Turkey by Imakofset

Photographs
p. i: Looking out over the Cloghoge Valley at Luggala; p. ii–iii: The ancient monastic site at Glendalough, seen from the road through the Glendasan Valley.

Contents

Routes

Map of Route Start Points

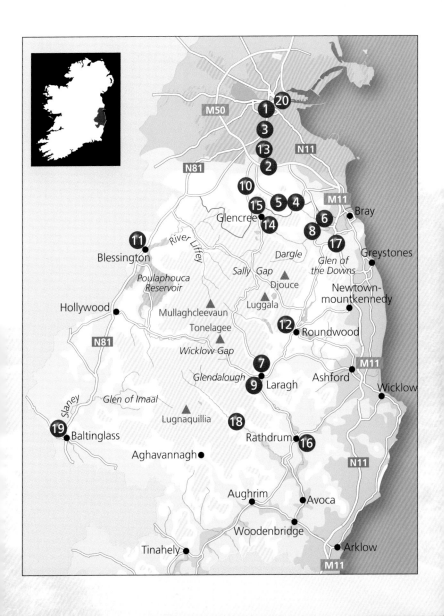

M50

N11

N81

Bray

M11

N81

Blessington

River Liffey

Glencree

Dargle

Sally Gap

Djouce

Glen of
the Downs

Greystones

Poulaphouca
Reservoir

Hollywood

Mullaghcleevaun

Luggala

Newtown-
mountkennedy

Tonelagee

Roundwood

Wicklow Gap

Glendalough

Laragh

Ashford

M11

Wicklow

Slaney

Glen of Imaal

Lugnaquillia

Rathdrum

Baltinglass

Aghavannagh

N11

Aughrim

Avoca

Woodenbridge

Tinahely

Arklow

M11

Quick-Reference Route Table

No.	Route	Grade	Distance
1	St Stephen's Green to Marlay Park	1	14km
2	Marlay Park–Glencullen Loop	2	19km
3	Rathfarnham–Glencree Loop	2	46km
4	Sally Gap–Luggala Loop	3	50km
5	Glencullen–Laragh Circuit	3/4	84km
6	Enniskerry–Wicklow Gap Circuit	4	112km
7	The Shay Elliott Memorial	3/4	52km
8	Enniskerry–Glen of the Downs Loop	2/3	30km
9	Glendalough–Glen of Imaal Circuit	4	74km
10	Cruagh–Glenasmole Reservoir Loop	3	23km
11	Blessington Lakes–Manor Kilbride Loop	2	36km
12	Roundwood–Vartry Reservoir Loop	2	45km
13	The Scalp–Sugar Loaf Loop	2/3	48km
14	Glencree–Crone Wood Loop	2	39km
15	Glenasmole–Seefin Circuit	3	38km
16	Rathdrum–Avoca Circuit	3	34km
17	Little Sugar Loaf to the Sea	4	67km
18	Aghavannagh through Tinahely Loop	4	60km
19	Baltinglass–Hollywood Circuit	4	84km
20	1998 Tour de France in Ireland Stage	5	185km

Acknowledgements

For me, cycling in the peace and solitude of the rolling countryside of the south Dublin foothills and the wild terrain of the Wicklow Mountains, which makes up the main routes of this guide, has often been a solitary experience, as this enhances the sheer pleasure and feeling of escape that comes with it.

Over the years that cycling pleasure has been further enhanced by the good company and enthusiasm of Ger Hartmann, Daniel Day-Lewis, Peter Crinnion, Fred Murray, Paddy Heaney, Paul Perry, Aidan Brosnan, Mary Hanlon, Niamh Kissane, Donal O'Sullivan, sometimes the spirit of Shay Elliott, and in the beginning my brother Donal, the original pioneer of these roads.

To my publisher, The Collins Press, for the initial encouragement and patience throughout. And in memory of my grandmother Una Charleton, for first turning the key that unlocked the door to this cycling kingdom.

The old bridge at Laragh.

Introduction

The thing about being born at the foothills of the Dublin Mountains is that they enter your subconscious at an early age and never let go. From an early age I used them as a playground of sorts, thanks chiefly and fortunately to devoted grandparents who took us mostly willingly on Sunday walks up and around places like the Sugar Loaf, Djouce Mountain, and the Hell Fire Club.

At school in De La Salle Churchtown I sat in many a classroom that looked directly out at the Dublin Mountains, and can remember becoming increasingly lured by a longing to escape into them, either by foot or any other means. When I started running as a teenager this opened up another avenue, as most Sunday mornings we would set off from Marlay Park and run up through Cruagh Wood and back, or sometimes all the way through Glencullen, where after many years abroad and in the city I returned to live. It was by bicycle, however, that the Dublin Mountains truly revealed themselves in all their openness and glory, and by natural extension, the Wicklow Mountains, the largest continuous upland region in Ireland.

When long-distance runs in the mountains became a little more of a chore than a pleasure, the bicycle at first proved a worthy substitute and now, I think, a superior one. The distances are far more manageable and far less limited, and there is something uniquely intimate about cycling on mountainous or hilly roads, certainly a step closer to Mother Nature and all her seasonal personalities.

Another part of that discovery, and unique to the Dublin and Wicklow Mountains, is that they are served by the historic Military Road, which runs some 58km from Rathfarnham in south Dublin to Aghavannagh in south-west Wicklow, with a side arm from Enniskerry to Glencree, and also from the Sally Gap to Roundwood.

It was constructed between 1801 and 1809, in the aftermath of the 1798 Rebellion, where the inaccessibility of the Wicklow Mountains had proved a problem for the government forces.

Captain Alexander Taylor of the Royal Irish Engineers was handed the task and the motivation was threefold: the road would enable troops to travel quickly to wherever they were needed; at the same time it would restrict the ability of the rebels to move unseen; there was also the fear of a potential French invasion on the east coast at this time, which would necessitate rapid movement of troops.

At first, any non-military personnel who wished to travel the route had to obtain a permit of transit from the Barrack Master in Dublin. Right from its early days, however, its blend of forested and mountainous and wild scenery was appreciated by anyone who got to travel on the road, and over 200 years later, the Military Road has lost precious little of its charm.

What has helped retain this charm is the fact so much of the area is part of the Wicklow Mountains National Park, some 20,483 hectares, the largest of Ireland's six National Parks. And all of which, naturally, lies on the doorstep of the capital city.

The essential purpose of this guide is to help cyclists of all abilities to explore the wonder and challenges that lie within the south Dublin and Wicklow area. Each route has been carefully selected to capture the foothills of south Dublin best and the true 'high' points of the County Wicklow, fondly known as the Garden of Ireland.

You will journey through some of the country's best-known tourist attractions, such as Glendalough and Luggala, and also to some hidden gems around the lesser-known roads along Kippure and Glenmalure and the beautiful Blessington Lakes. We will also visit the stage of the 1998 Tour de France that started in Ireland – Day Two of which raced through the heart of the Wicklow Mountains and finished in the Phoenix Park.

Now living on one of the exact borders of the Dublin/Wicklow Mountains, in the village of Glencullen, I am familiar beyond words with many of these routes, and my hope is that this guide can provide you with some surprising insights and useful tips, mined from over a decade of cycling in the area, even to those who may have cycled some of these roads before. It is through this often tranquil wonderland of sorts that these routes traverse, each with their own appeal and level of difficulty.

The aim then is not just to explore some of best the routes of the Dublin/Wicklow Mountains, but also the history, geography and archaeology – while also providing some useful tips along the way.

Enjoy, and happy and safe cycling!

How to use this book

Grading

The routes are categorised as follows:

1. The easiest graded mountain or hill cycles – short, gentle climbs, less than 30km.
2. Lower gradients, but distances can still be long.
3. Hilly routes that include some flat sections.
4. Steep hills over short distances or steep climbs over long distances.
5. The most challenging, long distances with very steep gradients.

> Note: the gradient is calculated by the height gained, divided by the distance travelled, multiplied by 100. A height gain of 100m, say, over a 2km (2,000m) climb multiplied by 100 equals a gradient of 5 per cent. (100 ÷ 2,000 = 0.05 x 100 = 5 per cent.) Cycling downhill is said to have a negative gradient.

Many of these routes cross through remote mountainous areas so be aware that mobile phone coverage may be absent.

Although cycling, like running, is sometimes best enjoyed as a solitary experience, the best advice is to not cycle alone; if you do, always tell someone your route and expected time of return.

The map scale is provided, and can differ from map to map. Each map has a compass symbol for orientation. Main towns, villages, rivers, mountains, and national roads are given.

The start/finish points are marked, and all the routes are loop and/or out-and-back cycles, except for the first and last. Directional arrows are provided to point out the right route in case of confusion. The elevation bar is an exact reproduction of the elevation of the route and gives an easy-to-read picture of the number of hills involved.

Equipment

There is no absolute necessity to wear cycling shorts, jersey and other gear specifically designed for cycling, although once you have tried it, and appreciated it, it's unlikely you'll ever wear otherwise again: this includes proper cycling shorts, jersey, gloves and, of course, a helmet.

A helmet should always be the correct size for the wearer. It should be worn fastened comfortably but not loose or pushed far back on the head. It should bear the safety standard number CE EN 1078.

Clip-in cycling shoes (or cleats) aren't absolutely necessary but they are immeasurably more energy saving and comfortable, although they do take some getting used to. If in doubt, always clip out! Gloves are another vital piece of equipment in the colder months.

It can be both fun and informative to record your route, or check pre-loaded maps for directions. There are a variety of apps for your smartphone enabling you do this, including mapmyride.com, strava.com and viewranger.com

Almost as important as the bike is the pump. Don't leave home without one, and always carry a couple of spare tubes. If you're a long way from home and you get a puncture you will need to have a spare tube to replace the punctured one. To get the tyre off the wheel rim and replace the tube, you will need tyre levers, and to put air in your tyre after replacing the tube you'll need a pump.

It is good to have a basic set of tools for most of the important nuts on your bike. A multitool, which incorporates a set of Allen keys and screwdrivers, should be sufficient.

The most convenient way to carry your spare tube and tools is in a small saddle bag or the back pocket of your jersey. The pump will usually have a holder attached to the bike frame.

Bike fit

Like buying a new pair of shoes, you should always buy a bike that is the correct size for you. If your bike is too big or too small it will be uncomfortable to ride and can cause all sorts of unnecessary pain. When buying a new bike you have the chance to make sure it is the correct size.

The staff in any good bike shop will ensure that your bike is the perfect fit. However, don't rely entirely on the bike shop staff and go armed with some understanding of how you should feel on a bike that is the correct size.

The fit of a bike is related to the size of the frame, and the adjustment of the saddle height, the fore/aft position of the saddle and the handlebar position. A good rule of thumb for a roadbike with a crossbar is that when you stand astride it, you should have no more than 4cm clearance of the crossbar.

When pedalling, your legs should never feel overstretched (saddle too high) or scrunched up (saddle too low). A general guide to find the correct saddle height is to put your heel on the pedal and when your leg is at the bottom of the pedal stroke it should be more or less straight.

When cycling, the ball of your foot will be on the pedal and at the bottom of the pedal stroke your leg will have a slight bend in it.

Your arms should be sloping forward to reach the handlebars, but not stretched. Sitting on the saddle, you should generally be able to reach the ground with your toes. If, when you are on the bike, the saddle or handlebars have to be adjusted to their highest or lowest position to feel comfortable, it is possible that the bike frame size is too big or too small for you.

Safety

- It is essential to ensure your bike is in a roadworthy condition.

- Always be courteous and cycle with respect for others, whether other cyclists, pedestrians, drivers or anyone else on your cycling route. This helps maintain your safety and the safety of others.

- Always wear a helmet while cycling. However, it is important to remember that a helmet will be of limited benefit in the event of a collision with a vehicle so don't let yourself believe that you are protected from all eventualities just because you are wearing a helmet.

- Cycle on the left and keep in tight to the margins. Try not to wander into the middle of the road. However, you and another cyclist are legally entitled to cycle two abreast (except when overtaking when you should be in single file).

- Always look behind when starting, crossing lanes or turning.

- Always indicate, especially, leaving roundabouts. Raise your arm out at a right angle to indicate where you intend going. Cycle decisively and make your intentions clear to other road users by using hand signals when planning to turn. Think ahead, anticipate drivers' actions and catch their eye.

- There is a big difference between cycling on a quiet country lane and the centre of a busy town or city, but wherever you cycle it is important to think about your safety at all times. Ensure you are familiar with the Rules of the Road – they apply to cyclists also. In particular, refresh yourself with the specific rules for cyclists.

- Maximise your visibility to other road users. Wear bright clothing.

- Be alert to what's happening around you; don't wear earphones while cycling. Cycle well clear of the edge of the roadside or kerb – debris and drains at the road edge are a hazard – and never cycle on footpaths intended for pedestrian use.

- If cycling in a group, always warn any cyclists behind you of hazards ahead, such as potholes, parked cars, pedestrians, etc. Good cycling etiquette goes a long way.

Bike maintenance

Always check that your tyres are pumped hard enough. You can use a pressure gauge to see if they are within the recommended pressure range as written on the side of the tyre. This will read something like 60–110 PSI. However, if you don't have a gauge, just squeeze your tyre with your thumb and if it feels soft it is probably too soft.

If your tyres are soft the bike will be harder to ride. Also, if you hit a pothole you can easily get a puncture because the inner tube gets pinched against the side of the pothole. It is also advisable to give each tyre a quick look-over for any cuts or debris, nails or thorns lodged in the tyre.

To prevent a build up of dirt and grime on your bike you should clean it periodically; a dirty bike will never ride as well as it should, nor indeed will the rider.

A bike should be washed down with hot soapy water. Take care to remove dirt from all of the awkward places. The best way to reach this dirt is by using cleaning brushes which are available from most bike shops.

When cleaning the chain and sprockets, it is best to use a degreasing liquid which will break down any build-up of oil and dirt and makes it easier to remove. An old toothbrush can be used for this job. Special chain-cleaning devices can be used, which pull the chain through a reservoir of degreasing fluid and then through a set of brushes to remove the dirt.

Once the bike is clean, dry it off with an old towel or cloth and then lubricate the chain, and the chain rings, both front and back, plus the front and rear gear-changing mechanisms.

Lightly spray oil onto the chain on the rear sprockets while turning the pedals slowly to ensure the distribution of oil all along the chain. Be careful not to spray oil onto the wheels or tyres.

As you spin the pedals, change the gears up and down a few times so that the oil is also distributed onto all of the sprockets. Spray some oil onto the joints on the gear-changing mechanisms also. Use the oil sparingly – it shouldn't be dripping off when you've finished. If you've applied a bit too much oil, wipe it off with a cloth.

Climate

Irish weather is naturally unpredictable. It is a good idea to bring a small knapsack with raingear. There are light, back-hugging knapsacks available.

Sunglasses and/or a visor are very important for sunny days, even in winter because the sun is low in the sky and can be blinding.

Useful contacts

Weather Forecast: for weather forecasts, check the Met Éireann website (met.ie) or www.mountain-forecast.com. The accuweather.com app also provides good information.

Weather Dial:
Munster 1550 123 850
Ulster 1550 123 853
Leinster 1550 123 851
Connacht 1550 123 852
Dublin 1550 123 854
Sea Area 1550 123 855

Emergency Services: for all emergencies dial 999. This includes Gardaí, ambulance, fire brigade, mountain rescue, coastguard. You can also dial the EU number 112, which connects to the same services. This number can be dialled in all EU countries. Both numbers are free of charge.

National Parks: the Wicklow National Park features prominently in many of the routes. See www.wicklowmountainsnationalpark.ie/

Websites
There are over 400 cycling clubs with 26,000 members in Ireland affiliated to www.cyclingireland.ie

– Facebook: https://www.facebook.com/cyclingireland
– Instagram: @cyclingirelandfed
– Twitter: @irecyclingfed
– YouTube: Cycling Ireland

Other useful websites are:

www.bikescheme.ie
www.boards.ie/cycling
www.cycleNI.com
https://cyclist.ie
www.discoverireland.ie
www.dublincitycycling.ie
www.irishcycling.com
www.leavenotraceireland.org
www.mbi.ie
www.mountainbiking.ie
www.mtbireland.com
www.stickybottle.com
www.trackcycling.ie
www.trailbadger.com
www.womenscycling.ie

For a very detailed glossary of bicycle- and cycling-related terms have a look at this website: www.sheldonbrown.com/glossary.html

Maps & Guidebooks

Ordnance Survey Ireland
Tel: 01 802-5379; e-mail: mapsales@osi.ie; website: www.osi.ie

EastWest Mapping
Tel: 053 9377835; e-mail: info@eastwestmapping.ie; website: www.eastwestmapping.ie

1. St Stephen's Green to Marlay Park

St Stephen's Green – Ranelagh – Goatstown – Sandyford – Marlay Park

Location: Dublin

Distance: 14km

Duration: 1 to 1.5 hours

Grade: 1

Height Gain: 108m

Verdict: Easiest route from the city to the Dublin foothills.

Cycle path approaching Marlay Park.

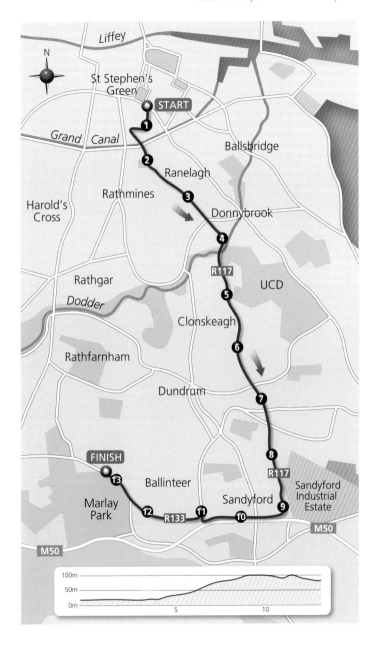

Start/finish

St Stephen's Green in Dublin city centre. There are several car parks nearby and on-street disc parking.

Marlay House.

This route is about crossing the doorstep from the capital city and out towards the largest continuous upland region in Ireland. It is not the only way from the city centre to the foothills, but certainly one of the most convenient, and perhaps even the straightest. And for the purpose of this guide, those foothills will begin at Marlay Park, which is not so much a starting point in itself as it is a rendezvous point.

The city centre starting point is St Stephen's Green, and from there the route heads south along Earlsfort Terrace. Turn right onto Adelaide Road, then left onto Charlemont Street, heading in the direction of Ranelagh.

Continue over the canal and along the Ranelagh Road all the way through the old village itself, after which the road becomes Sandford Road. The route continues straight, passing the turn left into Miltown, and continues up the Clonskeagh Road all the way up to the crossroads at The Goat Grill, in Goatstown.

The cycle path now appears. Follow this – again, straight all the way – up the Drummartin Link Road until the next main crossroads, where the Beacon Hospital and Sandyford Industrial Estate will be on the left. Turn right, following the cycle path as it goes left through the side of the Moreen Estate, and then exits left through a small gap in the wall that borders the motorway; once through that, you will be on the slip road that runs parallel to the M50.

Turn right, and simply stay straight on the cycle path for another 3km or so, passing through the junction with Ballinteer Road, onto the side of Brehon Field Road, and finally Grange Road. The main entrance to Marlay Park and the lower car park will soon appear on the left, well signposted.

However, if you choose to arrive by car, the top car park is better suited as a starting point into the foothills, which simply means turning left onto Grange Road when Marlay first appears in front of you. Follow this road for about 500m and then turn right onto College Road, and after another 500m or so, the top car park will be on your right.

Exiting Marlay Park top car park, with Montpelier Hill in the distance.

2. Marlay Park–Glencullen Loop

Marlay Park – Tibradden – Pine Forest – Glencullen –
Barnacullia – Ticknock – Marlay Park

Location: Dublin

Distance: 19km

Duration: 1.5 to 2 hours

Grade: 2

Height Gain: 357km

Verdict: Gentle teasing hills, rewarded with stunning views over the city.

The descent through Glencullen Valley.

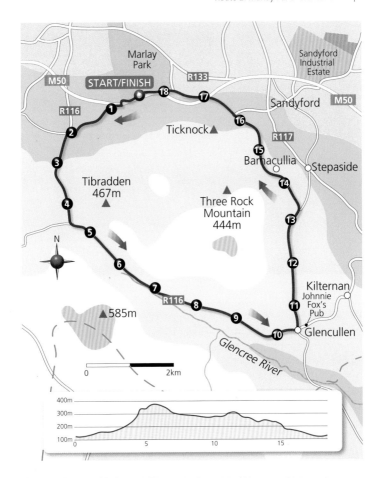

Start/finish

Marlay Park on College Road, south County Dublin. Easily accessible from Dundrum, Rathfarnham and from the M50: take the Dundrum exit, and follow the signs towards Ballinteer. At the first junction with Marlay, turn left, then take the next right. The top car park is about 300m down College Road on the right. There is ample parking space but take note of closing times, especially in winter.

The Blue Light Pub at Barnacullia.

For as long as I can remember Marlay Park has been my entry point into the Dublin Mountains, either running or on my bike. It is a great rendezvous point, an accessible and also central point of access to the Dublin foothills, and beyond.

It is a beautiful park and where I did many of my long-distance runs as a youngster, joining up most Saturday and Sunday mornings with Dundrum-South Dublin Athletic Club. But that's a lifetime ago.

As a starting or meeting point, what is popularly known as the 'top' car park at Marlay, situated on College Road, is about as good as it gets. It is the start of this gently appetising route into the foothills and the fringes of the mountains, but rewarding nonetheless, still one of my favourite routes either early or late in the season, or very late on a summer evening, when the sun is still going down over west Dublin, creating beautifully red-tinted skies over the mountain horizons.

Coming out of the car park, take an immediate right onto College Road, and after a short little descent, take a sharp left under the M50, briefly joining up with Whitechurch Road.

Now facing the small roundabout, take the second exit left onto Tibradden Road. The first exit leads up Kilmashogue Lane, a dead-end, so avoid that.

Tibradden Road turns gently around to the left, leaving the buzz of the M50 behind, with a very gradual ascent. There's a left turn up Cloragh Road which is also to be avoided, and instead it's a sharp right next, into the brief hollow of Mutton Lane.

Then comes a severe left turn, which usually necessitates stopping and unclipping from the cycling shoes, if wearing them. The entrance to Rockbrook College is also situated at this junction, but the left turn is onto Cruagh Road, and from here the climbing soon begins.

Avoid the right turn onto Mount Venus Road (the house opposite used to be a police barracks) and stay straight, as far as Cruagh graveyard, where the road forks – the original Military Road to the right, our road to Glencullen gently off to the left.

After another gentle hollow, the climb soon begins. I've run and cycled this hill hundreds of times, and it never gets any easier, but it gets you there nonetheless. Some turns are more severely ramped than others, but nothing a steady pace can't handle. It's a quiet road at the busiest of times, sometimes the only sound being the dogs barking from the nearby animal shelter back down on Mount Venus Road.

The road soon levels out with a sharp right turn over the stream that flows from Tibradden Mountain, to the left. This is the peak of the route at around 340m. About 50m later it's a sharp left, onto what's known locally as the Pine Forest Road, or the Ballybrack Road. Cruagh Road continues straight on, but that's for another route.

Here the route passes the Zipit at Tibradden Wood, popular for families with young children, while the road steadily climbs again, to 387m, the highest peak of the route. I've also cycled this stretch of hill hundreds of times and the funny thing is, it *does* get easier, sometimes only a few pedal spins out of the saddle are necessary to ease you up the top.

Then it's a gentle descent along the Ballybrack Road towards Glencullen, a lovely spin in any season, with a few gentle corners to heighten the thrill of the ride. About halfway down on the left is O'Connell's Rock, of significant local importance, where, on 23 July 1823, Daniel O'Connell, The Liberator, staged one of his monster meetings while campaigning for Catholic emancipation.

O'Connell's daughter Mary later married Christy FitzSimon, of the FitzSimon family who were of Norman origin and once owned the entire Glencullen Estate. O'Connell was present at a meeting in Glencullen House on 8 February 1823 when the idea of forming the Catholic Association, the organisation to secure Catholic emancipation, was first discussed.

This stretch of road is also lined with stone walls similar to those found in the west coast of Ireland: so abundant was the area in granite, it once provided employment for hundreds of stonecutters and quarrymen, while supplying large chunks of granite for many of the most important buildings in Dublin.

Soon the Ballybrack Road leads gently straight into Glencullen itself, (which translates from the Irish *Gleann Cuilinn* as 'valley of the holly'), the road briefly sharing with the Wicklow Way (which then turns right down Boranaraltry Lane). On the last noticeable bend on the right is Stars Of Erin

At the junction with Cloragh road on the Tibradden Road.

GAA club, which despite its proximity to Dublin, must be one of the most scenic grounds in the country.

At Glencullen crossroads, it's a left turn at Johnnie Fox's, famed as the highest pub in Ireland, and of course worthy of a stop for a coffee, or something stronger (it will be revisited on longer routes too).

The route now climbs, up Red House Road, then down towards Ballyedmonduff, but look out for the next left turn at the junction known as Cannons Corner, and the leafy shade of Taylor's Folly, the road now just about wide enough to accommodate two cars, so ride with care.

Soon the Blue Light is passed on the left, the pub with arguably the best view in Dublin, and also finest porter available outside of St James's Gate. The panoramic view opens out across Killiney Hill and Dublin Bay and the painted outline of Howth Head, and that first startling vista over the city, spread out below, in perfectly epic miniature.

The road then drops down through Barnacullia – *Barr na Coille* or 'top of the woods' – across the face of Three Rock Mountain, down Woodside Road, to the junction at Lamb Doyle's, where it's a left turn over the M50 on Blackglen Road, before one final left turn back onto College Road, and on to Marlay Park

Marlay is worth exploring in more detail, if time allows: the 247-acre park is overlooked by the historic 18th-century Marlay House, originally called The Grange, built by Thomas Taylor, whose son and grandson held important political positions from the 1740s to the 1760s. The name Taylor is still strongly associated with the area.

It was then purchased in 1764 by David La Touche, of French Huguenot origin, the first governor of the Bank of Ireland and member of the Irish Parliament, who extended it and renamed it Marlay, having married Elizabeth Marlay, daughter of the Right Rev. George Marlay, Bishop of Dromore. After exactly 100 years, it was sold in 1864 to Robert Tedcastle, the well-known Dublin coal and heating merchant, whose family lived at Marlay until 1925. It was then acquired by Philip Love, a market gardener, and at the time the largest tomato producer in Ireland. Love also bred racehorses, including Larkspur, who won the Epsom Derby in 1962.

In more modern times Marlay House was purchased by the former Dublin County Council, in 1972, and then opened it as a public park three years later. It was restored in 2000 and now open to the public for tours from March to May.

3. Rathfarnham–Glencree Loop

Rathfarnham – Mount Venus – Killakee – Glencree – Glencullen – Cruagh – Rathfarnham

Location: Dublin/Wicklow

Distance: 46km

Duration: 2 to 2.5 hours

Grade: 2

Height Gain: 809km

Verdict: Gentle climb over the Featherbeds into Wicklow's first glen.

Dublin city from the viewing point at Killakee.

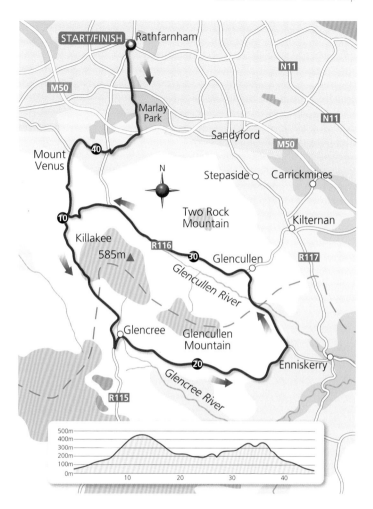

Start/finish

Rathfarnham village, south county Dublin. If coming from Dublin city centre, take the Harold's Cross road and follow the signposts to Rathfarnham. Also easily accessible from M50, taking the Dundrum or Firhouse exits, and following the signs for Rathfarnham. Ample on-street disc parking in and around the village.

T his route brilliantly captures some of the best roads and climbs that both Dublin and Wicklow have to offer in one fell swoop and is a perfect teaser for some of the longer routes to come.

The starting point in Rathfarnham village is in fact the beginning of the Military Road, almost 60km of undulating road all the way to Aghavannagh, deep the heart of the Wicklow Mountains.

Completed in October 1809 in the wake of the 1798 Rebellion, the road was built specifically to assist the British army in their search for the insurgents, many of who were hiding out in the Wicklow Mountains at the time.

Coming out of Rathfarnham, turn right at the Yellow House pub (the original inn located on that site actually popular with those insurgents, one of whom, Michael Dwyer, is thought to have frequented the place even while on the run. Rathfarnham was the scene of some skirmishes in the early days of that rising).

Rathfarnham church (the Church of the Annunciation) will be on the left, surrounded by some impressively large redwood trees. This road continues as the R115. After about 600m the road forks, at the suitably named Tuning Fork pub (now closed), and this route veers left, onto Whitechurch Road.

From there, continue straight on, passing the rear of St Enda's Park, to the crossroads at Taylor's Lane. Again, stay straight and continue to the small roundabout behind the Grange Golf Club, and taking the first exit, which will take you up Whitechurch Road and along the leafy wall on the rear side of Marlay Park.

This road soon leads under the M50, and then facing a small roundabout, take the second exit (left) onto Tibradden Road. (The first exit leads up Kilmashogue Lane, a dead end, so avoid that one.) Tibradden Road then turns gently around to the left, the hum of the M50 now receding in the distance. Next, it's a sharp right into the brief hollow of Mutton Lane.

Then comes a severe left turn (which necessitates stopping and unclipping from the cycling shoes, if wearing them). The entrance to Rockbrook College is situated at this junction, but the sharp left turn is onto Cruagh Road.

Almost immediately there is the right turn onto Mount Venus Road (the house opposite used to be a police barracks), which cuts across the Rockbrook area. Mount Venus cemetery is passed on the left, then the animal shelter and rescue centre, and on close inspection, the last remnants of the entrance to Mount Venus House, once a magnificent home, the last ruins of which are now used for farming purposes.

After about 1km it's a sharp left turn onto the old Killakee Road. Now the climb begins, gently at first, then very suddenly the road begins to ramp up towards the entrance to the Hell Fire Club, which sits so impressively atop Montpelier Hill, although it is not actually visible from this stretch of

32

road. Also passed on the left is the interesting Beehive Cottage, the original gate lodge to the once-grand Killakee House, the centrepiece of Massy Estate, now almost completely lost, first to partial demolition, then to the ravages of time.

The road continues to ascend steadily, a few bends helping to ease the way, before it levels out at the junction with Cruagh Road, on the left. This is one of the most popular viewing points over Dublin city, and on a clear day, especially in winter, the Mourne Mountains, some 100km away in County Down, are clearly visible.

Staying straight on the Military Road (R115), there's a quick switchback to the right, then left, before the route heads along the left side of Killakee Mountain, or White Sands Mountain, as it was once called. It's still a steady climb, the effort soon rewarded with the first panoramic view across the Glenasmole Valley to the west, and beyond that the first glimpse of Kippure mountain.

Popularly known as the Featherbeds, it is startlingly bleak, surrounded on both sides by peat bog land. In late spring and early summer, however, you can see how it earned its name, as the dramatically white bog cotton comes into bloom, decorating the entire area in a welcoming bed of seemingly perfectly white feathers. For many years my dad cut our own turf in this area, just off to the left, but that lonesome art has by now almost completely ceased here.

The ascent from Killakee, with Kippure mountain in the distance.

The highest point of this section of the Military Road, 480m, is then reached, and one interesting distraction on the left is the Lemass Monument, about 50m in from the road: this is the spot where the body of Noel Lemass was found in 1923, a Republican unofficially executed by forces of the Free State Government. His younger brother, Seán Lemass, also a veteran of the 1916 Rising, went on to become Taoiseach, from 1959 to 1966.

After a brief zigzag to the right, then left, the road straightens out again, and with that reaches the Dublin/Wicklow border – identifiable by the sudden change in the road surface, from smooth to slighter rougher. It's then a straight road down towards Glencree Valley, then dropping into the right, then left again, before the first meeting with the Glencree Road (the L1011), which veers off sharply to the left.

Take this sharp turn, which soon leads into the old Glencree Barracks: this was one of five barracks built along the Wicklow Military Road, and survives largely intact to this day. It has served a number of purposes over the years. After some 40 years in military service, in the 1840s the building became a government store; the Ordnance Survey also used it as a base for a while, and it was also used by the Post Office.

In the 1850s a dark chapter in its history began, as for the next 100 years it housed an industrial school run by the Irish Christian Brothers; these schools were established in Ireland under the Industrial Schools Act of 1868 to care for 'neglected, orphaned and abandoned children'. By 1884, there were 5,049 children in such institutions throughout the country. In 1945–46, German refugee children escaping the war were also accommodated here. Today the barracks is used as a Centre for Peace and Reconciliation, along with other exhibition rooms. There's also a café, perfectly welcoming for cyclists as a nice stopping point, even on a relatively short route such as this.

After a couple of sharp bends, the road then drops into the heart of the 5km-long Glencree Valley. Also passed here, on the left, is the fascinating German Military Cemetery, still neatly kept as a commemoration to the 134 Germans who either died in Ireland or whose remains were washed up on these shores during the two world wars.

The road surface along this stretch of the Glencree Valley – known as 'the sunny side' – can be rough in parts, so better to take it steady, and enjoy the views on the right of the valley and of the recent plantations of the old Irish oak tree, for centuries native to the area. The route gently rolls through the areas of Tonygarrow and Cloon, where the road briefly crosses paths with the Wicklow Way, then gently down into Curtlestown, with the pretty St Patrick's Church on the left.

After dropping down towards Kilmallin, there is a turn to the left, at about 21.5km, which heads back towards Glencullen. After a sharp climb followed by a descent to the Glencullen Bridge – and the border back over between Wicklow/Dublin – the road then hits the infamous Devil's Elbow, just under 1km long, before averaging around 10 per cent upward gradient.

There is another dip and a rise before entering Glencullen. To the left, just before the final climb, is the best point to view the original Glencullen Estate: the house itself is a Neoclassical-style villa designed by the famous Irish architect Francis Johnson, whose other notable works include the General Post Office and Nelson's Pillar on O'Connell Street (before it was bombed).

The FitzSimon family lived in the house until the early 1900s when it was sold but was later bought back by 'the Colonel' Manners O'Connell FitzSimon in 1953 who lived here until his death in 1985.

Daniel O'Connell's daughter Mary later married Christy FitzSimon, of the FitzSimon family, who once owned the entire Glencullen estate, and where O'Connell was present on 8 February 1823 when the idea of forming the Catholic Association was first discussed. Though a Kerry native, O'Connell had strong links with Glencullen, and would have visited Johnnie Fox's pub, founded in 1798, in its earliest incarnation; given that my house was once part of the Glencullen estate he might have visited it as well.

After passing the gates to Glencullen House, the road then reaches the crossroads, where we turn left. It is a straight 5km stretch along the Ballybrack Road (R116) up towards Cruagh Mountain, a gentle climb and then a sharp descent to the junction with Cruagh Road. Stay left here, and continue back up past the entrance to Cruagh Forest, and back around the meeting point at Killakee. From there it's a mostly downhill stretch, retracing the same route back across Mount Venus Road, down by Tibradden, and on into Rathfarnham.

The descent from the Dublin Mountain Featherbeds, towards Glencree.

4. Sally Gap– Luggala Loop

Glencullen – Glencree – Sally Gap – Luggala – Glasnamullen – Old Long Hill – Enniskerry – Kilternan – Glencullen

Location: Dublin/Wicklow

Distance: 50km

Duration: 2.5 to 3 hours

Grade: 3

Height Gain: 978km

Verdict: Tough but spectacularly scenic ride through a variety of majestic mountains, lakes and forests.

Passing McGuirk's Cottage on the climb towards the Sally Gap.

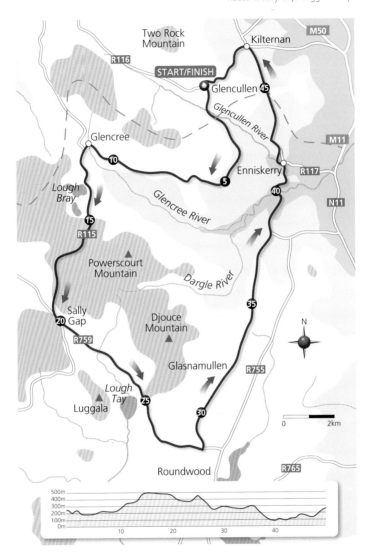

Start/finish

Glencullen in south County Dublin, where there is usually no problem
finding parking. Be careful not to block church/pub access, etc. Easily
accessible from the M50, taking the Kilternan/Carrickmines exit, following
the signs to Kilternan, then turn right at the church and follow the steep
incline up to Glencullen.

On the last day of January 2012, I packed several boxes into the back of my Jeep Wrangler, drove the 40km-odd into the Wicklow Mountains and across the Sally Gap, then checked into a small cut-stone cottage in the heart of the 5,000 acres of outer remoteness that is the Luggala Estate.

It was an Arctic cold winter's morning. My family reckoned I'd survive no more than a month, my friends said no more than a week. Instead, I survived more than a year, each day dreaming I had woken up in another world or another lifetime or somewhere in between.

To first enter Luggala, wrote Seamus Heaney, 'you do cross a line into a slight otherwhere' – and by that he also meant a part of the world not just separate from most others, but so magically timeless and unspoilt to be considered a world apart.

That is, and always will be, my first thought when Luggala comes into view on this route – and the indelible memories of the time spent living there. It wasn't about any self-discovery, but simply discovering a little more self-reliance, some shift away from the over-reliance on the various boxes and devices that have penetrated most of our lives, starting with the television.

So when the chance to live in Luggala presented itself there was no hesitation: it is its own miraculously preserved kingdom of nature that by turns of the hour or light can be touchingly calm or tortuously bleak, with sounds or silence to follow suit, the only certainty being it will never remain the same.

In winter, it could be the river whispering in my ear, or the wind heaving under iron clouds. The view from the half-door could be all space whitened by snow, while below, the shivering dark edges of Lough Tay could mimic the icy shores of the Arctic.

Or in summer, when the sun leaned in with laughter from across the openness, still warming the golden-

Memorial to Jim Stynes, Dublin and Australian rules footballer, at Lough Bray Upper, en route to the Sally Gap.

fleeced gorse and the sweet blooming ferns, it could be a jungle, the traces of 18th-century farmland and ancient paths buried under the miracle of growth that is the Cloghoge Valley in scorching July.

Or at any time, the eye could be drawn across the lofty Fancy Mountain of crumbling lunar granite, startled again by it, or to the scatterings of native Irish oak and giant Umbrella pine, the herds of Sika deer roaming beside the beer-coloured streams, and over to the bulking tip of Scarr, all seemingly beyond the limits of society.

The only road that runs parallel to Luggala (R759) – known locally as The Murderin' Pass – offers superb views of the estate and its surrounding valley in near entirety, including a glimpse of Luggala Lodge, for several generations owned by the Guinness family, nestled among the trees just north of Lough Tay and its white sandy beach – which coincidentally or not gives the perfect impression of a freshly pulled pint of Guinness.

Despite its apparent remoteness, it is far and yet so near: trace a simple trail of the geography of south Dublin and into north Wicklow, Glencullen is the first valley, Glencree the second, with Luggala just the third valley over. Still it does, naturally, take some effort to get there.

This route starts out from Glencullen. At the village crossroads, with Johnnie Fox's pub on your right, take the left turn onto Barrack Road and on down the steep Devil's Elbow, crossing the county boundary from Dublin into Wicklow at the Glencullen Bridge.

The road then promptly ramps up before gently descending its way towards Glencree: stop at the junction, and once the road is clear, veer right into Glencree (L101). Go straight ahead for about 4km, the road all the while subtly and yet laboriously climbing.

After reaching the bend in the road at old Glencree Barracks, the route then veers left onto the Military Road (R115) and with that the long, slow climb up towards the Sally Gap. The climb starts in earnest not long after McGuirk's Cottage, passed on the left, which also marks the pedestrian access point to Lower Lough Bray, part of which is privately owned, and houses Lough Bray Lodge, a summer villa-style home originally built in 1826 by Dr Philip Crampton, surgeon general to forces in Ireland.

McGuirk's Cottage was once open to the public as a teahouse, a favourite spot for walkers and writers, including John Millington Synge, who spent some time in Glencree in his early years. It is also the last building or habitation of any sort on this stretch of the Military Road until far down in the valley of Glenmacnass.

From here the road turns briefly to the right, then gently twists and climbs steadily, up towards the view out over Upper Lough Bray, down to the right. Like any climb of this distance and gradient, it is about riding at your own pace, and indeed pleasure. There is one sharp kick at the end of the climb, when the road turns sharply around to the left, and that's the worst of it over.

If totally out of breath (which is understandable), it's worth pausing to view the memorial stone to Jim Stynes, just off to the left, before the road completely levels and straightens out again: Stynes was an All-Ireland minor football winner with Dublin in 1984, before moving to Australia and becoming one of the most decorated and celebrated players in the history of Australian rules football. He died of cancer in 2012, aged 45, his ashes spread over this area, which he described as his 'treasured spot'.

Stay on the Military Road as the route now passes along a sort of plateau, and the entrance to Kippure Mountain is soon passed on the right. In 1960, this was chosen as the best location for the country's first television mast, which would distribute the signal of the newly formed Telefís Éireann.

From here the mountain vista truly begins to open up, the summits of Carrigvore and Duff Hill appear straight ahead, and off to the left appears Mullaghcleevaun, which at 848m is Wicklow's second highest mountain.

To the left of the road here is the moorland area of Powerscourt Mountain, and after about another 1km along the flat plateau, the road passes over the Liffey Head Bridge, where about 1km off to the left is the source of the River Liffey, stemming from a number of peat-stained pools. From here the river runs down the side of the Kippure Valley, on into Kildare, back into Dublin city, before entering the Irish Sea.

This is the highest point of the route, 525m above sea level, before the road drops slightly towards the Sally Gap. At the crossroads, turn left down towards Luggala (R759). There are a couple of teasing climbs again, before Lough Tay comes into view.

The road then runs parallel to a small section of forest on the right, then turns sharply right and ramps severely up onto The Murderin' Pass, where on the left Luggala reveals itself in all its glory. This stretch of road is both narrow and undulating and best ridden with considerable care, especially given the distraction of the stunning scenery off to the side.

After reaching the last sharp peak on the road, with the rear entrance to Ballinastoe on the left, the route drops suddenly and rapidly down past the Pier Gates entrance to Luggala Estate, and on towards Roundwood. Again, ride with care, especially at weekends, when cars are often parked across the road from the Pier Gates, on the left, and also on the right, where the Wicklow Way heads down towards Lough Dan.

The route is still descending when it reaches a crossroads: Roundwood is off to the right but this route turns left, along the 'old' or Long Hill road. If you miss the turn and reach the main Roundwoood Road (R755), after about 150m, you've gone too far – so simply turn back.

It's a calmly refreshing stretch of road, soon passing the front entrance to Ballinastoe and on towards Long Hill, with sweet views out to the Irish Sea to the right and up towards Djouce Mountain on the left. After another dip and then climb, with the Great Sugar Loaf briefly providing the backdrop on the right, the view opens up magnificently, out across north Wicklow and south Dublin, including Killiney and Sorrento Point and the serene Dalkey Island.

The road then falls rapidly down towards Enniskerry, veering left at Ballybawn (R760), then veering right around the edges of the Powerscourt Estate, before another left turn up towards the village itself, and the area known as Lovers' Leap. After passing the main entrance to Powerscourt Estate on the left, the route half bypasses Enniskerry, by taking Forge Road, on the left, then exiting the village (via the R117) on what is known as the 'back road', out by Knocksink Wood.

After that gentle climb, it's a straight spin through The Scalp and back on the Enniskerry Road towards Kilternan, before taking a left turn at the petrol station, just before the church, and then up the last little stinging climb on Ballybetagh Road (R116) and to the starting point at Glencullen village. This is a route that adds up to immeasurably more than the sum of its parts.

Lough Tay, Luggala, in winter, on the descent towards Roundwood.

5. Glencullen–Laragh Circuit

Glencullen – Pine Forest – Killakee – Sally Gap – Glenmacnass – Laragh – Oldbridge – Luggala – Sally Gap – Glencullen

Location: Dublin/Wicklow

Distance: 84km

Duration: 3.5 to 4 hours

Grade: 3/4

Height Gain: 1,492m

Verdict: Spectacular route through the very heart of the Wicklow Mountains.

Entering Glencullen Valley on the Ballybrack Road.

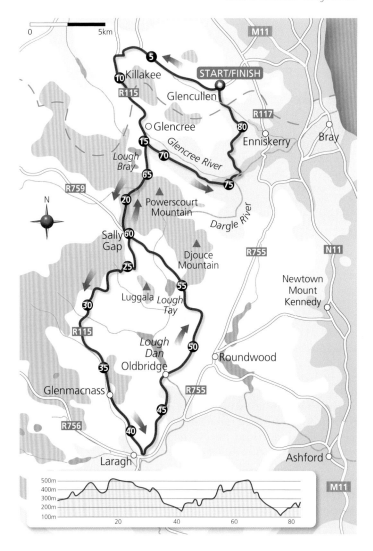

Start/finish

Glencullen in south County Dublin, where there is usually no problem finding parking. Be careful not to block church/pub access, etc. Easily accessible from the M50, taking the Kilternan/Carrickmines exit, following the signs to Kilternan, then turn right at the church and follow the steep incline up to Glencullen.

Depending on the time of year, or indeed time of day, it is possible to cycle long stretches of Wicklow's Military Road without passing a single person, either in a car or on a bicycle.

One such day in early June, a few years ago, having turned left at the Sally Gap and riding up towards Luggala, I suddenly saw another cyclist on the road ahead of me, tearing up the steep incline with a hardy look of determination – a sort of cross between Bill the Butcher from *Gangs of New York* and Daniel Plainview from *There Will Be Blood*.

He passed me in a speedy blur but a couple of minutes later I was thinking the resemblance had been a little too uncanny; later, when riding back up from Laragh, I passed him again, this time realising it was indeed Daniel Day-Lewis.

It was about a year since he'd won his second Oscar, for his role as Daniel Plainview, and riding in the Wicklow Mountains like this was his way of retreating from all the trappings that usually come with success like that.

I flagged him down to say hello and we ended up sharing the few miles back through Laragh, and he was thoroughly enjoyable company, recalling how cycling had always been his thing, especially in the early days in London, where he would ride around to various auditions, often showing up with splashes of bicycle oil on his hands and face.

Although by then into his 50s he looked superbly fit, which, of course, anyone would be if they cycled regularly through the heart of the Wicklow Mountains, as this route takes you.

Covering 84km, with six different climbs and a total elevation gain of 1,492m, it is certainly more marathon than sprint, and like any long-distance effort, it is all about setting your own pace.

As with Route 4, the starting point is Glencullen village, only this time heading out on the Ballybrack Road (R116), into Glencullen Valley, down towards Pine Forest Road, then veering left onto Cruagh Road. At the viewing point, it's a sharp left onto Killakee/Military Road (R115), and from there the slow, steady climb over and across the Featherbeds.

After dropping down into Glencree, continue on up the Military Road, the steep climb alongside Lower and Upper Lough Bray, and onto the plateau that runs alongside Kippure, to the left, and Powerscourt Mountain, to the right, also similar to Route 4, before this route takes on a life of its own.

On reaching the Sally Gap, this route now continues straight on over the Military Road, and from here, the next almost 20km is a stretch of seemingly endlessly winding and undulating road all the way down past Glenmacnass waterfall and then on into Laragh village.

As is quickly established, the Sally Gap is a bit of a misnomer, as there is no obvious sign or indeed sense of an actual 'gap'. This route was one of the two original east–west passes through the Wicklow Mountains (the other goes over the Wicklow Gap), and the two together certainly

The Glencullen Valley road towards Cruagh Wood.

provide a sort a gap between Kippure and Powerscourt Mountain and the edges of Djouce, now left behind, and the face of Carrigvore and Luggala Mountain and the rounded top of far-off Tonelagee, which now lie in front.

It must be one of the most exposed and lonesome but also exhilarating stretches of road in the country, a vast amphitheatre of moorland and mountainous landscape and scatterings of loose granite, in between stands of modern forestry plantations, often completely impassable in winter, yet surprisingly warm and sheltered on the finest of summer days.

Crossing over two rivers – first the Cloghoge, then the Inchavore – this stretch of road was not always as remote as it is now: about 3km south of the Sally Gap, there are remains of an old mountain house to the left of the road, some of the surrounding stone walls still intact; further on, after the sharp bend in the road that marks the meeting first with Carrigshouk and then Mullaghcleevaun just beyond, there are remnants of an old hunting lodge, also just off the road to the left, mostly now buried under sheets of moss. The spot is nonetheless easily identifiable by the presence of a few scatterings of Scots pine.

Soon the road gently descends down along the east bank of the Glenmacnass River, then plunges quite dramatically when it reaches the Glenmacnass waterfall, which drops some 80m into the flat green valley

The twisting incline up the Murderin' Pass at Luggala.

below. From here, it is a gently winding stretch of road into Laragh, and the junction with the main road from Roundwood (R755) and the road to Glendalough (R756).

The Glendalough Green café at the small triangular green at this junction is one of the most popular rest spots for cyclists, with its calm view across to Derrybawn Mountain. At about 41.5km, this also marks a sort of halfway point, and well worth a rest.

Now the route essentially heads back to Glencullen, but avoids the main road into Roundwood, and instead takes the sharp left, no more than 20m on the R755 coming out of Laragh, and from there climbs up over Laragh East to Oldbridge, crossing paths with the Wicklow Way, and offering fine views to the right out across to Trooperstown Hill.

At the Oldbridge junction, stay right (the left turn leads up to Lough Dan and a dead end). It's a bit of a climb from here, following the road above Roundwood, and Upper Ashtown to where the road meets the R759. Here, turn left back up towards Luggala. This is probably the most difficult climb of the route, with an average gradient of 5.3 per cent.

When the road eventually peaks and then levels out, the view down over Lough Tay makes it worthwhile. This approach also offers the best view of Luggala Lodge and its distinctly Gothic style of design.

Still best described as a Guinness estate, its history runs far deeper. Luggala Lodge has only ever had eight owners, at least from its earliest recorded date of 1788, when Peter La Touche, part of the wealthy Irish banking family of French Huguenot extraction, purchased a lease on the land and what was then a primitive hunting lodge 'for three lives [lifetimes] at an annual rent of £39', and rebuilt it in the style known as Strawberry Hill Gothic, named after the Twickenham villa dated from 1749.

It passed to three more generations of the La Touche family, then to the two generations of the Wingfield family, the then Viscount Powerscourt, before the Guinness family first showed their interest. Ernest Guinness (one of the few family members truly dedicated to the brewing business) began renting a part of Luggala around 1912, his love of the place perhaps partly explained by Lough Tay.

When his daughter Oonagh married for the second time in 1937, to Lord Dominick Browne, Ernest purchased Luggala and immediately presented it to her as a wedding present, so beginning the most celebrated period of its history – her hosting of parties for Irish musicians, actors and artists, combined with what poet John Montague described as her 'very dangerous sense of fun', earned the place a unique reputation entirely fitting with the landscape itself.

From there, in 1970, it was passed on to her son, the Hon. Garech Browne, also a direct descendant of Arthur Guinness, who likewise retained it as a place of entertainment, albeit a select one.

When the road passes down by Lough Tay, on the left, a small domed stone temple can be seen just next to the lake, which marks the burial spot of Tara Browne, Garech's younger brother, who grew up in Luggala, later swapping it for London, only to be killed, instantly, when he crashed his light-blue Lotus Elan at the age of 21. A month later, John Lennon was reading a newspaper report of Tara's death, at the EMI recording studios on Abbey Road, touched the piano keys and came up with opening line: 'I read the news today, oh boy, about a lucky man who made the grade ...' That song, 'A Day in the Life', provided the climactic track on *Sergeant Pepper's Lonely Hearts Club Band*, and the rest is Beatles' history.

It's another demanding climb back to the Sally Gap, then right onto the Military Road back down past Upper and Lower Lough Bray. When reaching the junction at Glencree, turn right in Glencree itself, follow the road all the way back down to the junction at Kilmolin, and from there swing left again back up through Ballybrew and the Devil's Elbow to the finish at Glencullen.

6. Enniskerry– Wicklow Gap Circuit

Enniskerry – Glencree – Sally Gap – Glenmacnass – Laragh –
Wicklow Gap – Blessington Lakes – Ballysmuttan – Kippure –
Luggala – Old Long Hill – Enniskerry

Location: Wicklow

Distance: 112km

Duration: 4.5 to 5 hours

Grade: 4

Height Gain: 1,933m

Verdict: Proper endurance test with continuously worthy reward.

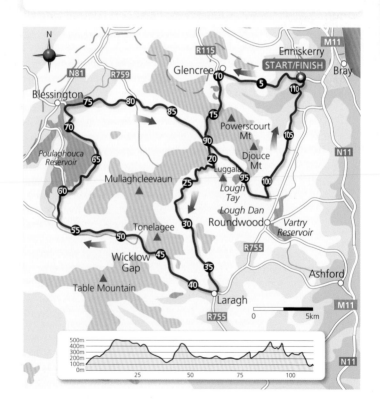

Start/finish

Enniskerry village in north County Wicklow. There is plenty of free off-street parking in and around the village, although it can be very busy on Sundays. Coming from the M50 (southbound)/M11, take the Enniskerry exit and simply follow the road (R117) up to the village.

The junction at Lockstown Upper, turning right towards Blessington Lakes.

On the first turn south-west out of Carrick-on-Suir, on the Tipperary/Waterford border, there's a suddenly steep climb known locally as the Seskin, which Seán Kelly would have ridden countless times en route to becoming the best cyclist in the world.

One day in early spring, a few years back, I travelled to Carrick-on-Suir to interview Kelly, who suggested a short spin out along the foot of the Comeragh Mountains might be a good way to warm things up, before the interview proper.

Of course, it sounded like a great idea. I didn't realise that Kelly wasn't one to hang around and feel sorry for properly amateur cyclists such as myself. On the approach to Seskin, my first question still rambling, Kelly instinctively shifted into a suitably low gear before accelerating seamlessly into the climb, leaving me dragging my back wheel. Within a few metres he'd opened a gap. A quick glance up and there was Kelly smiling to himself, still getting a little kick at outsmarting another rider.

Coming towards Ballyknockan and the view towards Blessington Lakes.

Of course, it soothed my bruised ego when we later worked out he'd by then cycled almost 1 million km, nearly 25 times around the world. And that his 22 classic wins make him by that standard the fourth most successful cyclist of all time after Eddy Merckx (50), Bernard Hinault and Jacques Anquetil (both 29).

Kelly retired in 1994, thus ending the Kelly–Stephen Roche era that had put Ireland at the centre of the world cycling map, and riding with him that day was a lasting reminder that success on the bike comes not just from talent, hard work and steely determination but also a fair amount of skill.

It's a nice way of introducing this route, one of the longest of this guide, and which essentially begins with a suddenly steep climb, out of Enniskerry village, up towards and then into Glencree Valley. For the opening 14km (along the L101 onto the Military Road) it's a mostly uphill gradient, rising from 91m to 527m, the average uphill gradient being 3.1 per cent.

After veering left at Glencree onto the Military Road, it's up past Lower and Upper Lough Bray, on towards the Sally Gap, and from there the long, winding and beautifully remote stretch of the Military Road on down past Glenmacnass and into Laragh.

Here's where things get interesting: at the small triangular green next to the cafe and the meeting with the R755 and R756, the route veers right in the direction of Glendalough, for just under 2km, before veering right again in the direction of the Wicklow Gap. (The R757 continues the short distance into Glendalough, where it reaches a dead end.) The ancient monastic site that is Glendalough is considered one of Ireland's most beautiful visitors' destinations, and most popular: it's not, however, suitable for cycling, but certainly worth a visit on foot whenever time might allow. At this point on the route, however, it's best to keep going.

So begins the climb up the Wicklow Gap, coming some 38km already into the route, climbing steadily for almost 8km, to 458m, with an average uphill gradient of 4.3 per cent. It's got the feel of an Alpine climb, the rider slowly emerging out of the treeline and onto the exposed road, going steadily upwards all the while, leaving the valley below. Off to the left there's a glimpse of the old lead mines and down to the Glendasan River, and on the right is Hillside House, but most of the concentration is instead on the road ahead.

The climb up from the Sally Gap towards Luggala.

The Sally Gap in winter.

There is a nice respite about halfway up, where the road briefly levels at a viewing point on the left, back down towards the valley. That might be the back of the climb broken, but there's still another long, hard drag before the top of the Wicklow Gap – again a not particularly discernible 'gap' – which lies at 458m, with another viewing point, and the turn-off to the Turlough Hill Reservoir

From there it's a beautifully rolling descent, with Fair Mountain on the left and Tonelagee to the right, over the Glashaboy Bridge and then the Ballinagee Bridge, and on towards Hollywood.

Then comes the gentle right turn towards the Blessington Lakes, and the R758, at about 56.5km, easily missed if not alert to it. Taking the road into Lockstown Upper, the road rises gently before descending again just as the lakes come into view.

It is then a sharp right, at almost exactly 60km, onto the lake drive road, into Ballyknockan and on up towards Lackan. This road seems to drag on and on, but it is constantly rewarding nonetheless, with teasing views left across the still lake waters.

After passing by Blessington Bridge on the left at about 73km, the route continues to wind on for another while towards Manor Kilbride, before taking a sharp right at Oldcourt, at about 76.5km, then up towards Ballysmuttan.

After another short but testing climb, the road then drops down again towards Kippure, crossing over the River Liffey at Ballysmuttan Bridge, now named in honour of Ciarán Jones, the Garda who died tragically here during flooding in October 2011.

Shorty after crossing there's a quick climb up to the junction with the R759, where the route turns right up towards Kippure, with the old sand pits now visible just off to the right. After passing the entrance to Kippure Holiday Village, the climb begins in earnest, almost 9km in all, with a 3 per cent average uphill gradient, back up to the Sally Gap.

The view down to the right is interesting: known as the Coronation Plantation, in the shadow of Carrigvore, it was an ill-fated effort to forest this section of the upper Liffey area in 1831 by the Marquess of Downshire, who named the plantation to celebrate the coronation of the Sailor King, William IV, its broad scattering of oaks, pines, alders and rowan bearing a distinct resemblance to the African veldt, particularly in high summer.

After reaching the Sally Gap, the route continues down into Luggala, all the way to the junction with the old Roundwood road, at the R759, then taking the sharp left back towards Old Long Hill and the junction with the R760. From there it continues to wind and undulate along what is known as the back road into Enniskerry, past the entrance to Charleville demesne on the left, up to the entrance to Powerscourt Estate, then back down to the starting point in Enniskerry.

7. The Shay Elliott Memorial

*Laragh – Shay Elliott Memorial – Glenmalure – Greenan –
Rathdrum – Clara Laragh – Trooperstown – Moneystown –
Tomriland – Annamoe – Laragh*

Location: Wicklow	**Grade:** 3/4
Distance: 52km	**Height Gain:** 845m
Duration: 3 to 3.5 hours	**Verdict:** Suitably challenging tribute to Shay Elliott, plus scenic afters.

The old bridge at Laragh.

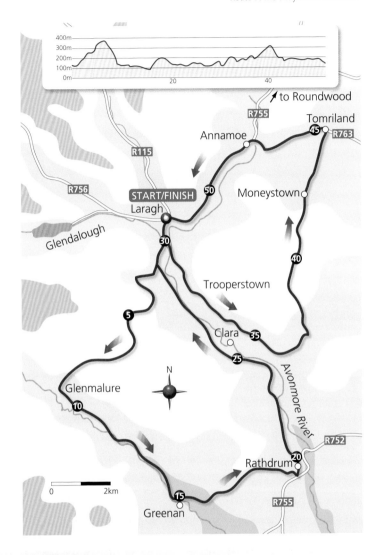

Start/finish

Laragh village in south County Wicklow. There is ample free parking in and around the village, including at Glendalough Green. The main access route by car is via the M11: take the Roundwood/Glendalough exit at Kilmacanogue, and follow the R775 into Roundwood, Annamoe, and then Laragh.

The descent towards Glenmalure with the Shay Elliott Memorial on the left.

Ask most cycling enthusiasts to name the first Irish rider to wear the yellow jersey in the Tour de France and chances are they'd go with either Sean Kelly or Stephen Roche. But they'd be wrong.

On 25 June 1963, Shay Elliott won Stage 3 of the Tour, from Jambes, in Belgium, to Roubaix, his 33-second victory margin enough to give him the coveted *maillot jaune*.

Elliott wore the leader's jersey for the next three days, and it would actually be another 20 years before the second Irish rider got to wear it: Kelly earned enough bonus points on Stage 9 of the 1983 Tour, which took the riders from Bordeaux to Pau, to take an overall one-second lead. He wore the jersey for one day – and despite his great career, never won it back again.

Although he was born in Dublin, this route is a fitting tribute to the somewhat forgotten Elliott. He did much of his training in the Wicklow Mountains, one of his favourite routes being the climb up between Cullentragh and Kirikee mountains, then down into Drumgoff.

He later lived in Kilmacanogue, before his tragic death on 7 May 1971, aged just 36. His story was the subject of the superb 2009 documentary, *Cycle of Betrayal*, which certainly informed me about just how great a rider he was.

Professional cycling rarely does fairy-tale endings, and Elliott's story presents all the glamour of professional cycling and at the same time, all the treachery of it. Some of the best archive footage in *Cycle of Betrayal* features clips of Elliott attempting his comeback, when he was three years out of the sport.

'It would take a lot to win back what I had,' Elliott said of his comeback, 'but from a personal point of view, I can win back a terrible lot.' That was the spring of 1970, and Elliott was 35 years old. His life up to that point was already extraordinary, a tale of rags to riches and back again. Growing up in Crumlin, the son of a motorbike mechanic, he only learned to ride a bike at the age of 14. Elliott achieved the previously unfeasible by breaking down a series of barriers – cultural and physical – to make it into the peloton.

In 1955, aged 21, he became the first foreigner to be ranked the top amateur in France. 'This Irish lad came to France to learn to cycle,' they said, 'but we think he has come to teach us.'

Elliott wasn't quite as romantic about it: 'Due to an ambitious curse, I think, I just wanted to go further afield.'

His reputation for courage, and class, earned him a place on the Helyett-Potin team, the best around, alongside French greats Jacques Anquetil and Jean Stablinski, the son of Polish immigrants. Although Stablinski became a dear friend, Elliott would eventually leave the team suspecting both riders of sabotaging his chances for victory, most infamously the 1962 World Championship, where he finished second to Stablinski. After 11 years as a professional, Elliott retired in 1967, actually the first English-speaking rider to wear the leader's jersey in all three major tours – the Giro (1960), the Vuelta (1962), and the Tour itself (1963).

Most riders would have lived off that for the rest of their lives, but Elliott returned to Ireland with only the same small suitcase he had left with. He had split from his French wife, Marguerite, and lost his entire life savings in a dodgy hotel investment in Brittany.

'Just one of those things,' said Elliott, 'that happens to somebody that's nice.'

Four years later, at the age of 36, he would be dead.

He'd started up a panel-beating business, which provided some refuge, but inevitably he missed cycling, and the lure of riding the 1970 World Championships in Leicester proved irresistible. This would be his comeback. Having sold his stories of sabotage and of cycling's drug-taking to the *People* newspaper, however, he found himself an outcast from the sport he once charmed. On the morning of 7 May 1971, two weeks after his father's funeral, Elliott was found in the small apartment above his business on Prince's Street in Dublin city centre with a gunshot wound to the chest, which had fatally ruptured his heart and liver, The coroner's report deemed it 'self-enacted'. Few of his close friends actually believe this, and instead claim it was a tragic accident. Either way, it was a sad ending to one of Ireland's greatest cyclists – a poignant remember of which comes at the first high point of this route, and the sight of the stone memorial just to the left of the road with the simple inscription: In Memory of Shay Elliott, International Racing Cyclist.

Starting out from Laragh, the route heads south, briefly taking the R755, the main road from Roundwood to Rathdrum. Crossing over the Bookey Bridge, with the original Derrybawn House off to the right, the route then takes the Military Road, which veers off to the right after about 1.5km, signposted Glenmalure and Aghavannagh.

So begins the climb, skirting the edges of Derrybawn Mountain, this first stretch part of the old Grand Jury road, which pre-dated the Military Road. It makes for about a 5.5km climb in all, with an average uphill gradient of 4.3 per cent, peaking close to the Shay Elliott Memorial, at 365m.

After passing over this high point – with a forest entrance and parking on the right – the view ahead opens up in all its glory, across a small spread of mountain summits, including Lugnaquillia itself, which at 925m is not just Wicklow's highest mountain, but also the highest mountain in Ireland outside of Kerry (which has several higher peaks, including the Big Daddy of them all, Carrauntoohil, at 1,039m).

The road then drops down into Drumgoff. In summertime this area is doused in deep green heather. The last section is one of the steepest, before the road reaches a junction (the Military Road continues straight, the right turn leads into the dead end of Glenmalure Valley, and the left turn heads back towards Rathdrum, which is the road we now take.

At this left turn is the Drumgoff Inn, and although a little early on this route, no more than 10km, worthy a stop for some refreshment. The original Drumgoff Inn dates back several centuries and early guests include the poet Thomas Moore in the 1820s and later, in 1924, British writer Evelyn Waugh.

This route then heads directly towards Rathdrum, following the Avonbeg River into Greenan, the site of a farm museum which presents exhibits going back over 100 years, when traditional hill farming used only the horse and donkey. The farm includes an interesting maze, planted in 1988, and also tearooms in the traditional farm cottage. From Greenan, the route veers right, skirting the edges of Ballyteige Wood, all the while following the signposts for Rathdrum.

On reaching Rathdrum, at about 20km, the route passes through the village and onto the main R755 road back towards Laragh. It's a beautiful stretch of road, at times a little narrow and winding, but well shaded and sheltered, passing through what is known as the Clara Vale Forest.

The route also passes by Clara Laragh Fun Park, on the right-hand side, following the Avonmore River, and then back into Laragh, passing the turn on the left that had first taken the route up to the Shay Elliott Memorial. Now, however, instead of continuing straight into Laragh, the route suddenly turns off to the right, just after the Bookey Bridge, and takes a long but nonetheless hugely rewarding detour right around Trooperstown Hill. There are a couple of testing climbs along this way, into Glenwood, where we turn left, just after 37km, and from there the mostly straight road over the Moneystown Bridge, with the hill at Castlekevin to the left, before coming to the Tomriland crossroads. Turn left at the crossroads into Annamoe, then right at the junction over the Annamoe Bridge, and back along the main R755 into Laragh.

It's a gentle enough ride back into Laragh, but at 52km, this route packs in a lot a punch, and is a fitting tribute to Shay Elliott.

The final descent into Drumgoff at Glenmalure.

8. Enniskerry–Glen of the Downs Loop

Enniskerry – Kilmacanogue – Glen of the Downs – Delgany – Greystones – Bray – Enniskerry

Location: Wicklow

Distance: 30km

Duration: 2 hours

Grade: 2/3

Height Gain: 402m

Verdict: Gently sweeping ride through Wicklow's small gem of a glen.

The clocktower monument in Enniskerry .

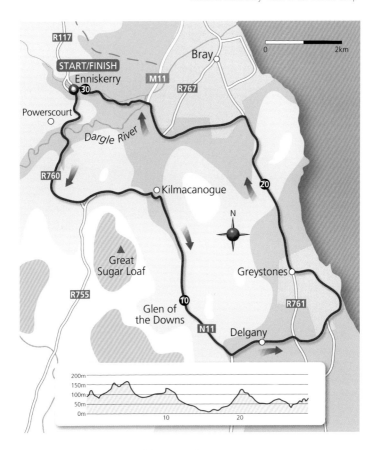

Start/finish

Enniskerry village in north County Wicklow. There is plenty of free off-street parking in and around the village, although it can be very busy on Sundays. The main access route by car is coming from the M50 (southbound)/M11; take the Enniskerry exit and simply follow the road (R117) up to the village.

The Glen of the Downs has long been known as one of Wicklow's original scenic routes, helping to earn the county its reputation as the Garden of Ireland and, indeed, the gateway into it.

Cutting through an almost 2km-long glacial valley, passing from Kilmacanogue to the north and into Kilpedder to the south, and rising on either side to about 250m, it is covered in a thick canopy of broadleaf trees

61

The N11 road through the Glen of the Downs.

– oak, cherry, rowan and ash – and, depending on the time of year, often deeply scented with honeysuckle or wild garlic.

However, some will say it's not quite what it used to be: back in 1997, in protest at the planned upgrade of the N11, which runs directly through it, a group of eco-warriors set up camp there, adamant that the roadworks would forever alter the very nature of the valley.

After nearly three years, the High Court eventually ruled their protest out of order, and the road upgrade was carried out, completed in 2003. The wider roadway probably has taken away some of the original magic of the place, although it is still a charming experience to ride through, even if means taking the short but busy stretch of the N11 itself. It's also now a designated nature reserve.

This route sets out from Enniskerry village, and takes the initially daunting climb up towards Powerscourt Estate, on the R760. It's a tough but short hill and things even out pretty quickly, before the road descends again, passing along the Powerscourt Estate to the right, and down to the Tinnehinch bridge.

Powerscourt is now one of Wicklow's top tourist stops, and worthy of a quick detour into the grounds on the estate for a view of the main house. There is a fee to visit the gardens, obviously not accessible by bike, but certainly worthy of a visit on another occasion.

It has a history in tune with its grand surrounds: the 1st Viscount Powerscourt was keen to assert his position in Irish society, and in 1730 set about transforming the medieval castle at Powerscourt into a grand mansion. He commissioned the German-born architect Richard Castle to build Powerscourt House, a 68-room Palladian-style mansion, completed in 1741. In 1961, the Slazenger family purchased the estate from the 9th Viscount Powerscourt, and in 1974 a major refurbishment of the house was completed in preparation for it joining the gardens as a visitor attraction.

Then disaster struck: in the early hours of 4 November 1974, a fire broke out on the top floor and by the following morning the main part of the house was a roofless shell. No one was injured, but all of the principal reception rooms and bedrooms were destroyed, leaving mostly original stonework dating back to the 13th century. It remained a burnt-out ruin until 1996, when the house was reroofed and then reopened to the public by then President Mary Robinson in 1997.

Leaving Powerscourt behind, the route takes the right turn just after the Tinnehinch bridge, staying on the R760, then sweeps around Ballyorney, down past Ballybawn Cottages and out to Rocky Valley, with the small peak of Carrigoona off to the left. From there it's a short descent into Kilmacanogue.

At the small roundabout, take the second exit (right), then turn left, which takes you across the N11 flyover. It's then right again (the second exit on the small roundabout) and down onto the N11, for the brief but busy run through the Glen of the Downs itself.

The Great Sugar Loaf, viewed from near Enniskerry.

Take the first exit left, signposted Delgany, and follow the R762 into the village. Continue along the main Delgany Road until the next roundabout. Take the second exit onto Mill Road, and from there on into Greystones.

The road sweeps around the left, with the seafront now appearing on the right. Go straight through the town on the Church Road, turn right onto Rathdown Road, then join the R761, following the signpost for Bray.

It is then a mostly straight and gentle climb in towards Bray, with some sweet sea views off to the right, and the Little Sugar Loaf providing the backdrop on the left. From here it's through the area known as Windgate, Bray Head now dominating the skyline to the right, and at the roundabout, take the first exit onto Bray Southern Crossroad. This takes us back in the direction of the N11, soon passing Kilruddery House and Gardens on the left, another popular tourist spot, with immensely important gardens, one of the last remaining 17th-century gardens in Great Britain and Ireland. Again, not suitable for cycling, but worthy of a visit on another occasion.

Approaching the N11, follow the R768 and onto the flyover, taking care here as it can be busy. After crossing over, take the third exit down onto the N11, for another brief stretch of main road, before taking the next exit left. From here it is a gentle and peaceful ride back up the R117 at Cookstown, past Kilbride Lane onto the old Bray Road, before arriving back in Enniskerry.

9. Glendalough–Glen of Imaal Circuit

Glendalough – Wicklow Gap – Hollywood – Donard – Glen of Imaal – Knockanarrigan – Mullin Cross Roads – Aghavannagh – Glenmalure – Glendalough

Location: Wicklow

Distance: 74km

Duration: 5 to 6 hours

Grade: 4

Height Gain: 1,484m

Verdict: A mighty long, undulating and brilliantly rewarding ride through Wicklow's heart.

Entrance to the main car park at Glendalough.

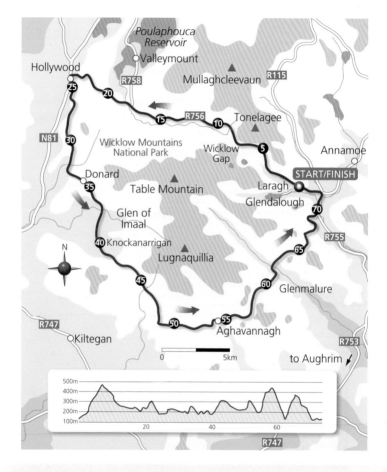

Start/finish

Glendalough in south County Wicklow. There are two main car parks adjacent to the main monastic site: there are charges in summertime, worth checking in advance (see: www.heritageireland.ie/en/midlands-eastcoast/glendaloughvisitorcentre/). There is also limited on-street parking. The main access route by car is via the M11, taking the Roundwood/Glendalough exit at Kilmacanogue, and following the R775 into Roundwood, Annamoe, Laragh, and then Glendalough.

A few years ago I met Greg LeMond for a cycle in west Clare. He arrived at Doonbeg Golf Club in the late afternoon. His transatlantic flight had been badly delayed and he had not slept in two days.

His wife and three children had arrived the day before and had gone off sightseeing, without, it seemed, leaving a note. And the first thing LeMond did was to start unpacking his bike.

He spread out the different parts in the main courtyard. Frame, wheels, handlebars, saddle. A few golfers passed by, looking bemused. Isn't that the famous American cyclist? Before Lance Armstrong came along? With one small wrench he assembled the bike in five minutes. 'LeMond' was written along the white frame and forks. He leaned it against the wall; it gleamed in the sunshine.

'Best way to deal with the jet lag,' he said with a smile. 'Go for a bike ride.'

The story of Greg LeMond's life. Best way to deal with his prodigious sporting talent? Go for a bike ride. Best way to handle his Attention Deficit Disorder? Go for a bike ride. Best way to cope with his fame? Go for a bike ride. Best way to recover from his near-fatal shotgun wound? Go for a bike ride. Best way to manage his depression? Go for a bike ride.

Then he paused for a second: 'Have you got a pump? I forgot my pump.'

The three-time winner of the Tour de France, the man who introduced professional cycling to the joys of time-trial handlebars, aeroframes, wind-tunnel testing, heart-rate monitors, Oakley sunglasses and Giro helmets, had forgotten his pump. I was tempted to say 'no' and let him ride on flat tyres. It might have evened things up.

I often think about that meeting with LeMond whenever driving to the start of a cycle, like this route: trying to remember everything to bring along is not a straightforward task, especially for a relatively long cycle such as this. There are the obvious essentials – helmet, pump and spare tube – but I've sometimes driven to the start of a cycle to realise I've forgotten my cycling shoes. And you're not going anywhere without those.

This route starts out from the main car park at Glendalough, on the R757. Originally known as the Seven Churches, Glendalough is now one of the country's top tourist spots and one of the most important monastic sites in Ireland. This early Christian monastic settlement was founded by St Kevin in the sixth century and from it developed the Monastic City, several ruins of which remain, including the 30m-high round tower.

This route soon starts climbing far higher than that, leaving the round tower and the rest of the ruins far down in the valley below as the road ascends towards the Wicklow Gap.

One quick glance at the profile of this route will tell you it's a tough spin, but I love it. with four pretty major climbs, four pretty minor ones, and a total gain of 1,484m, it feels longer and a little more exhausting than it actually is but also exhilarating, signing off with the sweet descent down the side of Derrybawn and into Laragh.

Coming out of the car park, turn right onto the R757 for a just a few hundred metres, then take a sharp left onto the R756 and on up to the

Wicklow Gap, Brockagh Mountain to the right and Camaderry rising to the left, all the while following the Glendasan River. Some of this road was covered in Route 6 (Enniskerry–Wicklow Gap Circuit) but after completing the climb and heading back down over the Ballinagee Bridge, the route stays on the R756 all the way into Hollywood, at about 23km.

Continue through the village towards the main N81, and then turn left for a brief spell on this road for just under a kilometre, before taking the first left off it, and from there along a lovely stretch of road which cuts calmly through the Hollywood Glen. Follow this road towards Donard, over what is known as the Hell Kettle Bridge.

On entering Donard, on Church Road, turn left, following the signpost for the Glen of Imaal, and over the bridge at Snugborough. The Glen of Imaal is still used as a military artillery range, and behind the bulking Lugnaquillia now comes clearly into view, which at 925m is the highest peak in Wicklow, and the highest anywhere in Ireland outside of Kerry.

Then turn right, at about 36.8km, on the road in towards Knockanarrigan (easily enough missed, so look out for the signpost). Continue straight through the crossroads at Knockanarrigan and after 500m or so veer right, over the Rustyduff Bridge, which crosses the Little Slaney River, and follow the signpost for Dwyer-McAllister cottage, which is soon passed on the road off to the right.

This was the scene of a famous shoot-out during the 1798 Rebellion, where rebel leader Michael Dwyer fought off the surrounding British troops and made good his escape over the snow-covered mountains. Following a fire the cottage lay in ruins for almost 150 years but was later restored to its original thatched form, built with stone from the locality and whitewashed inside and out.

The first ascent of the Wicklow Gap, from Glendalough, in the Wicklow 200.

The road then winds down to Ballinabarney Bridge. Stay left, and the road veers around to the right again. Stay on the road all the way down to the junction at what is known as Mullin Cross Roads, where a sweeping vista of south Wicklow opens up in front. A right turn would lead on to Rathdangan, but this route turns left and continues along the side of Slieveboy Mountain and in towards the bridge of Aghavannagh, which is where the original Military Road ended.

The imposing Aghavannagh Barracks is passed on the left, one of the six barracks built along with the Military Road and used for army purposes until 1825. The site then reverted to the landowner, William Parnell of Rathdrum, grandfather to Charles Stewart Parnell, and part of the building was used as a hunting lodge. In 1944, An Óige bought the property and it served as a youth hostel until 1998, and more recently has been restored again by its private owners.

After crossing the bridge and the River Ow, the road soon starts climbing again up over Slieve Mann to the left, Croaghanmoira Mountain to the right, briefly skirting along the Aghavannagh River. This is actually one of the toughest climbs in Wicklow. It is just under 4km to the pass, but comes on this route after 50km, with an average uphill gradient of 7.1 per cent, although it is usually well sheltered by the forest on either side.

Then it's a wonderful downhill into Glenmalure and the crossroads at Drumgoff. Just before the bridge, the remains of Drumgoff Barracks are visible on the right. It was used by the military until 1844, then leased to the Wicklow Mining Company for use as both office and living quarters. By 1868, mining had stopped in the valley, and the barracks site reverted to the landowner – the Kemmis family of Ballinacor House. Only a ruined shell of the building remains today.

Pass straight through the crossroads, with Drumgoff Inn on the right, then up the final climb towards the Shay Elliott Memorial on the right. The climb is just over 3km long, but has a 6.6 per cent uphill gradient. The instant reward is the sweet descent back to the junction with the R755, and left for the short ride back in Laragh. On reaching the village, turn left onto the R756, in the direction on Glendalough, and the last 1.5km back to the car park.

10. Cruagh–Glenasmole Reservoir Loop

Cruagh – Killakee – Glassamucky Brakes – Castlekelly Bridge – Glenasmole – Ballinascorney – Bohernabreena – Piperstown – Cruagh

Location: Dublin

Distance: 23km

Duration: 1.5 to 2 hours

Grade: 3

Height Gain: 554m

Verdict: Short city-skirting rollercoaster with suitably scenic thrills.

The descent at Glassamucky Brakes towards Glenasmole Reservoir.

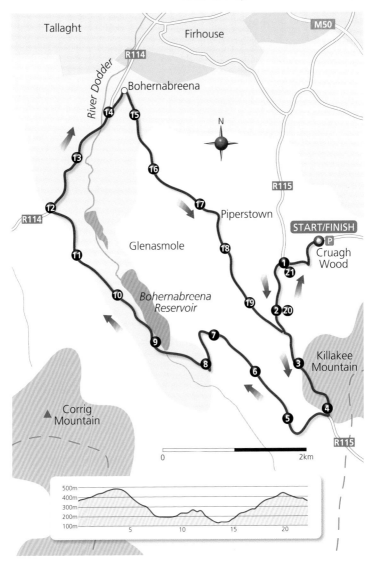

Start/finish

The car park (free) at the entrance to Cruagh Wood in south county Dublin. Note the early closing time in winter. The main access route by car is via the M50, taking the Dundum/Ballinteer exit and following the signs for Ballinteer.

After passing Marlay Park, take the R113 from the Kilmashogue roundabout, then the R116 up to Tibradden, staying right. The entrance to Cruagh is on the left. Also accessible from the Killakee Road (R115).

Most cyclists – including myself – are creatures of habit, usually preferring to stick with the tried and trusted routes, rather than venture too far into the unknown. For years I'd been cycling over the Featherbeds and on through the various gateways of Wicklow that follow without once ever veering down into the sheltered valley of Glenasmole and its two small reservoirs, even though it was right there for the taking.

That all changed recently when one of my cycling colleagues and old school friend Fred Murray alerted me to its pleasures: it's now one of my favourite short mountain loops, especially early in the summer, when there mightn't be much mileage in the legs. Because the valley is so sheltered it also comes into bloom a little earlier than the surrounding mountainous area, and is normally flush with sweet-smelling gorse from early May.

Glenasmole, as I later found out, comes steeped in legend too, mentioned in some of the epic tales of Fionn mac Cumhaill and the Fianna. In one tale, mac Cumhaill was kept captive under the spell of a witch in the hills above Glenasmole, and in another, he battles and then defeats the Dragon Glenasmole.

It is hard to imagine either of those scenes taking place in Glenasmole, as it is actually one of the quietest and most peaceful places in Dublin, a hidden gem that doesn't appear to get too many visitors beyond those enjoying the beautifully placid pathway around the reservoirs. It seems like a place a little lost in time but also in its own time, and largely unchanged in the last century, despite its relative proximity to Dublin. Some 5,000 acres of the area around Glenasmole, which had been taken over by

The view back towards Kippure, from Glassamucky.

NAMA, was recently bought by the state, thus preserving it for at least the foreseeable future.

The route starts – or again has its rendezvous – at the car park at Cruagh Wood, near the top of Cruagh Road. There is ample space although the car park closes early in the winter months (4 p.m.) so double-check that before setting off.

Coming out of the car park, turn left onto Cruagh Road, and continue around the bend at the top of Massey Estate and up to the viewing point, where Cruagh Road meets the road coming up from Killakee and, with that, turns into the Military Road.

Turn sharp left onto the Military Road, with the city vista far down to the right, which, like most mountainous views, is at its most dramatic in the winter months, when the far-off Mourne Mountains in County Down are easily seen on clear days.

There is now a gentle climb towards the Featherbeds, soon passing a turn down to the right, which leads to Piperstown: the route will later emerge from here, but for now go straight on over the Featherbeds, passing the Noel Lemass monument on the left, and then after about 4km, take the right turn down into the valley, marked R7236.

The turn is just before the Dublin/Wicklow border, easily marked by the sudden change in road surface (from super smooth to the roughly smooth): the road down into the valley is proper country, in places just wide enough for one car, so take care; although it is great fun, it is a bit like a short ski run.

After a bend in the road carry straight on, then veer left at the gentle fork in the road, down into the area known as Glassamucky Brakes. At the junction at the bottom of the hill, turn left – the right turn heads into the small hamlet of Glassamucky, the 'Green of the Pigs'.

Continue on past the scattering of stone cottages that make up Glenasmole, until reaching the Castlekelly Bridge, suitably marked, which crosses over the River Dodder not long before the river spills into the reservoir.

Turn sharp right just after the bridge (the road straight ahead being a dead end), and from there the road soon runs parallel to the first of the two reservoirs. These reservoirs were constructed in the 1880s; the first was designed to provide drinking water for most of the then south city suburbs, such as Rathmines, while the second provided water for the various flour, woollen and paper mills then scattered along the course of the river as far as Clonskeagh.

The road then dips gently before climbing again, running alongside the reservoirs down to the right, with Ballymorefinn Hill to the left, sheltered by a healthy cluster of large Scots pine. It is not a difficult climb but it requires some effort.

Continuing mostly straight, the road then drops again and meets the stop sign at the junction with the main R114. Turn right onto this road, into Ballinascorny Lower, with the entrance to the Dublin City Golf Club on the right.

The road then drops quite severely in towards Bohernabreena, passing the main front entrance to the reservoirs, again on the right. Continue straight and at about 15.5km turn right, signposted Piperstown, onto the Bohernabreena Road, passing St Mary's GAA Club and then a large cemetery on the left. Continue straight and stay left at the next fork in the road. There now begins a climb up through Piperstown and the back of Montpelier Hill. Ignore the next road and continue up the winding hill, which then rejoins the Military Road, although not before one last kick in the climb.

Turn left and head back down to the viewing point, swinging right onto Cruagh Road, and then down to the car park where the route started.

Road from Cruagh Wood towards Glencree in winter.

11. Blessington Lakes–Manor Kilbride Loop

Blessington – Boystown – Valleymount – Annacarney –
Ballyknocken – Lacken – Manor Kilbride – Blessington

Location: Wicklow/Kildare

Distance: 36km

Duration: 1.5 to 2 hours

Grade: 2

Height Gain: 340m

Verdict: Relatively flat loop of the lakes with near constant water vista.

The Downshire Monument and St Mary's Church on the main road through Blessington.

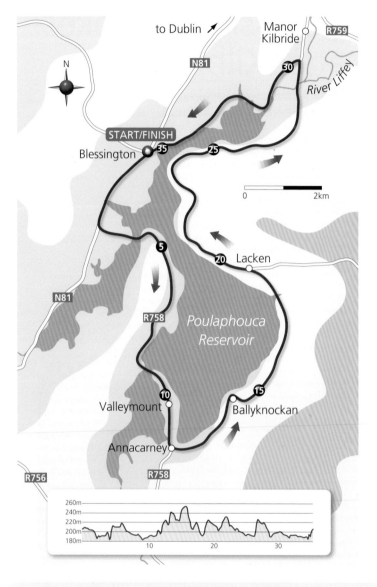

Start/finish

Blessington village, west County Wicklow, with its ample parking, is the starting point, situated on the main N81, southbound from Dublin.

Ruined castle on the road from Manor Kilbride, looking back towards Blessington.

Of all the routes in this guide, this one is perhaps the most equally captured – and indeed equally tempting – when cycling in either direction, whether that means starting out in a clockwise direction from Blessington, or anticlockwise.

Appearances, however, can be deceptive, because while it lacks any of the obvious climbs of most other routes in this guide, it is by no means an easy spin. Take a look at the profile: as if drawn by a drunken hand, it shakes slowly yet perilously up and down throughout. The elevation gain is 340m, with a maximum elevation of just 259m, but a good deal of the time will be spent out of the saddle, either when taking in the gentle inclines, or to simply gain a better view of the placid and often glistening reservoir.

Depending on who you ask, the area is either known as the Blessington Lakes or the Poulaphuca Reservoir. Officially the lakes are known as the latter. The reservoir was created between 1937 and 1947, when the ESB dammed the River Liffey at the waterfall in Poulaphouca, to the west, right on the Wicklow/Kildare border.

The entire lower valley area was flooded, the resulting lakes extending over approximately 5,000 acres. A small village was submerged and the remains of roads can still be seen leading down into the lake at various points along the route.

My preference is to ride anticlockwise, if only because it's the direction I am most familiar with – but given the largely circular route, the directions can be just as easily followed in reverse.

Either way, Blessington, with its ample parking, is the starting point, on the main N81. Straddling the Kildare border, to the west, it was a medieval town. One of its main visitor attractions today is Russborough House, about 5km outside the town, although not passed on this route.

Instead, this route travels about 2.8km out of the town in the same direction – south – past the industrial estate area, but then takes the first left off the N81 and onto the R758, which after about another 1km then passes over the water, and offers the first view proper out across the lake.

Continue along the R758 through Boystown Lower, then cross another bridge at Valleymount, past the school and the old post office, with calm views of the water on either side of the road.

The route then takes a sharp left onto the L4365, at about 11.5km, also known as the Lake Drive road, where the lake circuit begins in earnest, the road constantly rising and dipping. There's another fine view from Ballyknockan of the lakes, the mountains of Moanbane and Black Hill and, behind them, the bulk of Mullaghcleevaun providing the backdrop off to the right.

It is a slightly straighter ride before the road climbs gently again into Lacken, the road continuing to skirt the edges of the water. There is another bit of a climb before reaching what is known as Blessington Bridge, one of the main crossing points, at 24km. The route, however, continues on in the direction of Manor Kilbride, passing the old National Rowing Centre on the right. This point on the water is still a popular spot for rowers of all ability.

The lakes soon disappear as the road heads straight into Manor Kilbride, crossing over the River Liffey at Ballyward Bridge. Avoid the left turn soon after, but rather take the first left on reaching the village, heading back in the direction of the water.

There's another very gentle climb as the River Liffey comes into view again, on the left, and from there it is a pleasantly straight run back into Blessington, on the Kilbride Road, again passing the main bridge on the left, but not passing over it, entering the town at the junction with the N81.

Bridge over Blessington Lakes at Valleymount.

12. Roundwood–Vartry Reservoir Loop

*Roundwood – Tomdarragh – Tiglin – The Devil's Glen –
Ashford – Killiskey – Ballyduff Crossroads – Waters Bridge
– Newtownmountkennedy – Ballinashinnagh – Ballinastoe
Bridge – Roundwood.*

Location: Wicklow

Distance: 45km

Duration: 2.5 to 3 hours

Grade: 2

Height Gain: 726m

Verdict: Gentle but truly rewarding loop around water, forest and mountain.

The entrance to the Devil's Glen.

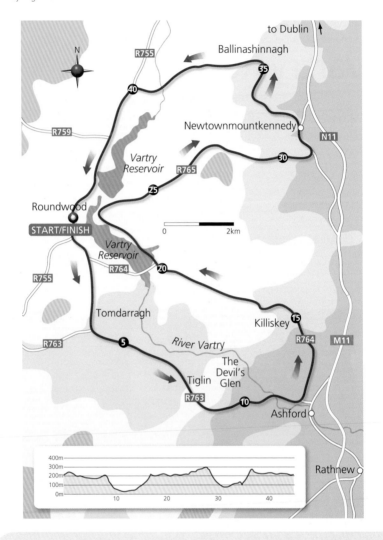

Start/finish

Roundwood in south County Wicklow, famed as one of the highest villages in Ireland. There is ample parking in and around the village. The main access route by car is via the M11: take the Roundwood/Glendalough exit at Kilmacanogue and follow the R775 into Roundwood.

For years Roundwood was considered – or, indeed, claimed – to be the highest village in Ireland, and although it's not far off, that honour rests with Meelin, in north Cork (still disputed, occasionally, by Glencullen, in south County Dublin). What is certain is that it's the highest in Wicklow.

At 238m above sea level (compared to Meelin's 251m) Roundwood also provides easy access to the mountainous routes to the west, and although this route heads east, it is still by no means the flatter side. The aim is to take in as much of Vartry Reservoir as possible, with a spin off into the surrounding hills for good measure.

For over 150 years already, the Vartry Reservoir has been cleaning and filtering the water supply to Dublin, originally with the aim of improving the health of the city by delivering an uncontaminated water supply, and today it's piped to a large open service reservoir in Stillorgan in the southern suburbs of Dublin and operated by Dublin City Council. Work on the reservoir began in 1862, when the lower reservoir was formed by the construction of an earthen dam across the valley of the River Vartry. The original, lower, reservoir was completed in 1863, and has a capacity of 11.3 billion litres of water; a second embankment was completed in 1923 to form the upper reservoir, which as a capacity of 5.6 billion litres.

Roundwood was historically known as Tóchar ('the causeway') and these days is a popular summer destination for campers and hikers during the summer months. It also has a close association with two former presidents of Ireland: Seán T. O'Kelly lived locally and Erskine Childers is

Waterfall at the Devil's Glen.

buried in the grounds of the Derralossary Church of Ireland church, just south of the village.

From Roundwood, the route begins by heading away from the village on the R755 in the direction of Glendalough, then swings left, onto the R763, with the Byrne & Woods restaurant to the left, and the hardware shop to the right.

It continues up for just a short distance and reaches another fork in the road. Keep to the right, in the direction of Tomdarragh (the road left continues as the R764). It's a calm, easy ride to the Tomriland crossroads, where we turn left onto the R763 in the direction of Ashford.

This stretch of road can be busy so ride with care, especially as it winds down past the Tiglin Adventure Centre, and up past the entrance to The Devil's Glen, one of the prettiest spots in Wicklow, no matter what the season. The road also passes through Glenmore, for years the home of Nobel Prize-winning poet Seamus Heaney, who first rented and later purchased a cottage there, mixing his time between Dublin and Wicklow.

On the descent again into Ashford, avoid the first left after coming over Nun's Cross Bridge, and take the next left, just at the top of the village, and from there the road heads north on the R764, towards Killiskey.

Stay straight though the next three crossroads, the second one being Ballyduff Crossroads, all the while heading back towards the Vartry Reservoir as the road loops through and around the edges of Carricknamuck, to the north.

At the next fork in the road, with the reservoir now facing you, stay right, as the road briefly passes over the water and back towards the R765 and Roundwood itself. Turn right at this junction, which heads down to Newtownmountkennedy, passing Roundwood Golf Club on the right, at about 27km, in Ballynahinch Upper.

As the road descends again into Newtownmountkennedy, it meets the junction with the R722: turn left and cycle up through the town on Main Street, staying straight up Church Road (ignoring the right turn which heads out towards the N11).

From here, it's a nice, winding climb up by Season Park, which we pass on the left, continuing through Cooladoyle, staying straight. Then turn left, where the road rises sharply again up towards Ballinashinnagh, and the Kilpedder Rifle Range. Continue straight over this pass to the Ballinastoe Bridge, then stay right until the junction with the R755 again. From there it's a straight and mildly undulating ride back into Roundwood, with plenty of views of the reservoir to the left.

This was one of my favour summer evening routes while living in Luggala, when in the mood to avoid some of the longer climbs, and it never once disappointed.

13. The Scalp–Sugar Loaf Loop

Marlay Park – The Scalp – Enniskerry – Cookstown – Ballyorney
– Ballybawn – Great Sugar Loaf – Kilmurry – Kilmacanogue –
Glencormack – Enniskerry – Marlay Park

Location: Dublin/Wicklow

Distance: 48km

Duration: 2.5 to 3 hours

Grade: 2/3

Height Gain: 751m

Verdict: A brace of neat little climbs around one of Wicklow's most famous mountains.

The road through The Scalp, towards Enniskerry.

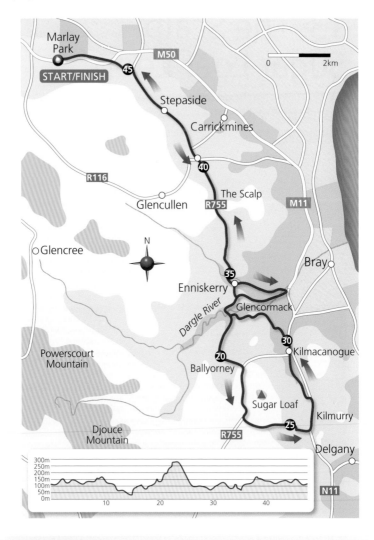

Start/finish

Marlay Park on College Road, south County Dublin. Easily accessible from Dundrum, Rathfarnham and from the M50: take the Dundrum exit, and follow the signs towards Ballinteer. At the first junction with Marlay, turn left, then take the next right. The top car park is about 300m down College Road on the right. There is ample parking space but take note of closing times, especially in winter.

No mountain dominates the skyline of the south Dublin/Wicklow border more than the Sugar Loaf, sometimes known as the Big Sugar Loaf, or more commonly, simply the Sugar Loaf.

At 501m it's far from being the highest peak in Wicklow, but many say offers the best views, especially on a clear day in winter, and better still as the sun comes up in the east.

Its appearance, at any time of the year, is of a volcanic-type mountain, topped with a scattering of sugary ash. In fact it's not volcanic at all, but an erosion-resistant deposit, the sugary coating composed of broken Cambrian quartzite. Its evenly steep slopes and relative isolation have given it a special place in the heart of the Wicklow landscape, and for that reason alone is worthy of its own loop in this guide. I've been cycling the 'The Sugar Loaf' loop since my teenage years, and it still provides the calm satisfaction that comes with skirting its bold edges.

This route begins at Marlay Park, again a rendezvous point as much as a starting point. From the top car park, turn left onto College Road, then a short distance to the junction with Blackglen Road, and from there straight on up over the M50 flyover to the Lambs Cross crossroads.

Turn right onto the Enniskerry Road, and then it's a straight ride up past Stepaside and Kilternan, through The Scalp, and down into Enniskerry village, staying left down Monastery Road.

Now, partly to warm up the legs, the route turns left, on entering Enniskerry, and down the R117, on the Bray Road, all the while skirting the edges of Glencullen River.

At the bottom of the hill, just before the road reaches the junction with the N11, swing right up the Cookstown Road, an oasis of calm despite being within sight and sound of the N11.

At the top of this road, the entrance to Powerscourt Estate faces you: turn left and down past Lovers' Leap Lane and over the Tinnahinch Bridge,

Exiting The Scalp on the road towards Enniskerry.

then veer right, towards Ballyorney, on the R760. Stay left after the road climbs again, and from there it's down past Ballybawn Cottages to the junction with the R755.

Left heads down to Kilmacanogue, but our route turns right, up the steepest part of this route, along the old Killough mines. It's a short but tough climb, reaching 290m, the highest point on this route.

Not far after the road levels out, with the Sugar Loaf now in close proximity on the left, take the first left turn at Glasmullen and into Glencap Commons South, which passes the main car park and entrance to the Sugar Loaf, again on the left.

This point offers the best view of the mountain, at its best in the late afternoon when the sun shines directly onto the broken Cambrian quartzite.

From here, the road soon descends again, down the L1031 past Calary Lower, to Kilmurray. The entrance to the Glenview Hotel is at the bottom of the hill, on the right, but the route stays left, onto Quill Road, which runs parallel to the busy N11, and into Kilmacanogue.

At the small roundabout, turn left for a very brief spell on the N11, then take the first exit left, at Glencormick, past the entrance to the Avoca shop and cafe.

From here, follow the quiet road back up through Glencormick and Little Newtown before rejoining the R760 and Charleville Demesne.

Just before re-entering Enniskerry, take the first left before the village, then cycle straight through the crossroads and take the back road out, known as Church Hill, passing the entrance to Knocksink Forest on the left. From here, it's back on the R117 to retrace the route through The Scalp, turning left at Lambs Cross crossroads and down to the starting point at Marlay Park.

The base of the Great Sugar Loaf from Glencap Commons South.

14. Glencree– Crone Wood Loop

Glencree – Aurora – Crone Wood – Old Long Hill – Ballinastoe – Rocky Valley – Coolakay – Onagh Bridge – Curtlestown – Glencree

Location: Wicklow

Distance: 39km

Duration: 2 to 2.5 hours

Grade: 2

Height Gain: 645m

Verdict: Gently winding and at times testing loop deep into the heart of Glencree Valley.

Part of the restored barracks at Glencree.

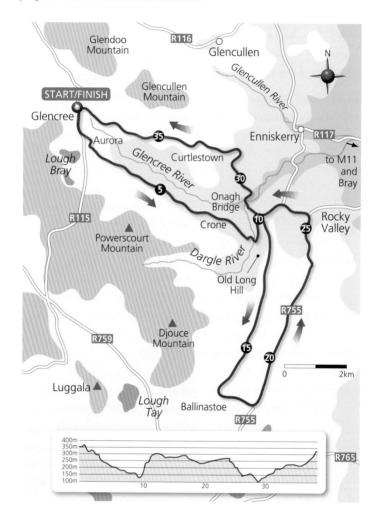

Start/finish

Glencree visitor centre in north County Wicklow. There is ample parking within the grounds of the centre, best accessed by car coming from the Rathfarnham/Dundrum direction, taking the R115 towards Killakee, and following the Military Road into Glencree. At the junction at the top of Glencree Valley, take the sharp left, and the Glencree visitor will be just a few hundred metres along on the right.

Monument to Liam Horner, Olympic cyclist, at Glencree.

There is something magical and mystical about the Glencree Valley. Trace the simple geography of south Dublin and it's just the second valley over from the city, yet it remains largely of its own time and place.

For centuries it was largely uninhabited too, the poor land, the steep rocky terrain and dense cluttering of small Irish oaks making it a somewhat unwelcoming place. The later development of the large private estates, such as Powerscourt, forced the local population further up into the valley, where they felled trees and marked out their plots with stone walls, developing the small townlands that exist today, such as Ballycoyle, Tonygarrow and Ballylerane, with plenty of old stone wall remnants as well.

Pockets of the old Irish oaks remain, along with a new plantation, known as the Millennium Oak Glen scheme, in Cloon. Just past the entrance to this forest park there is an inscription in an old piece of oak in memory of John Millington Synge, who spent many a lost hour wandering in the valley in his younger years. From his poem 'To the Oaks of Glenree' it says:

> *My arms are around you, and I lean*
> *Against you, while the lark*
> *Sings over us, and golden lights, and green*
> *Shadows are on your bark.*

John Millington Synge, 1871–1909

The name Glencree, *Gleann Crí*, most probably derives from *Gleann Criothaigh*, which would mean 'the shaking bog', and would certainly describe the upper western part of the valley.

This route starts out from the Glencree visitor centre, on the site of the old Glencree barracks (for more details on which, see Route 3), and like most other routes that's a rendezvous as much as a starting point, particularly if this route is being used as an extension/detour of any others that pass over the early stages of the Military Road. Don't be deceived, however: at just under 40km, it contains two of steepest inclines and declines in all of north Wicklow.

On exiting the Glencree visitor centre, turn left onto the L1011, where the road soon joins up with the Military Road (R115). Stay straight for another few hundred metres and then veer left down into Aurora, on the back road into Glencree, on the southern side of the valley. It's certainly more sheltered than the northern side of the valley and gets precious little sunlight in winter, which means it is liable to frost in cold weather, but a beautifully peaceful stretch of road nonetheless.

Another few hundred metres after turning left off the Military Road, on the left-hand side of the road is a small granite boulder, half-carved, with the inscription: *Liam Horner, Olympic Cyclist, 'the last prime'*.

The Great Sugar Loaf, from the top of Glencree Valley.

Liam Horner is not nearly as celebrated as Wicklow's favourite cycling son, Shay Elliott, but it's another worthy monument to the rider who in 1967, while still working as a carpenter, became the first Irish amateur to win a major race outside Ireland, with his victory in the Manx International on the Isle of Man.

He had ambitions to follow in Elliott's tracks, using these same Wicklow roads as his training base, out and back from his home in Monkstown. Horner never rode in any major tour yet racked up a stack of wins, including the Irish road race title in 1971, plus the Tour of Ireland the following year, and rode in both the 1968 and 1972 Olympics.

Horner, like Elliott, also died in tragic circumstances, in 2003, following an accident at work. He was renowned for attacking every *prime*, those intermediate sprints within a race, hence the inscription 'the last prime'.

The route winds down through Glencree, an incredibly dense green at the height of summer, with the Glencullen River hidden in the valley below. After passing through the old townlands of Ballycole and Ballyross and the entrance to Crone Wood on the right, the road drops and twists sharply, with the entrance to Powerscourt Waterfall at the bottom of the hollow.

The road climbs sharply again, then reaches the crossroads at Ballinagee, at about 10km. Here, turn right and up one of the steepest inclines in all Wicklow, so hold onto those handlebars!

There is some respite when it reaches the junction with the Old Long Hill road, where it's another right turn, and soon another sharp climb past the entrance to the car park for Djouce Woods. From the crossroads to the high point of Old Long Hill it's about 3km, averaging 5.6 per cent uphill gradient, although it is naturally much steeper than that in places.

Apart from another sudden and sharp dip in the road, it's a straight ride towards Ballinastoe woods and mountain bike trail. Just before the trail, however, turn left and down to the junction with the R755, running from Kilmacanogue to Roundwood.

Turn left again and stay on the R755 towards Kilmacanogue, on a mostly smooth but gently undulating road, before it drops suddenly again into Rocky Valley. Begin to slow down near the end of the hill, because the route then veers off left again, at Ballybawn Cottages, and back onto the R760.

From there continue straight, passing the road up to Old Long Hill on the left, then taking the next left, which turns back up towards Crone Woods, the road right heading back down to Enniskerry. Passing through Coolakey, the route arrives back at the crossroads at Ballinagee, only this time it turns right, and down the very steep decline, past the back of Powerscourt, to Onagh Bridge. This is a seriously steep downhill stretch and the road is not great in patches, so care is needed

At the bridge, turn right, through a magnificent canopy of trees, and follow the road as it winds left again up by Onagh, passing the turn to Glaskenny and the Knockree Youth Hostel on the left.

Stay straight until the road dips and then emerges again at the area known as Annacrivey, then take a sharp left back onto the L1011 in the direction of the Glencree visitor centre, passing through Curtlestown and the entrance to the Millennium Oak Glen scheme on the left. Back at the top of the valley, passing the German War Cemetery on the right, the route returns to its starting point at the Glencree visitor centre.

Road down from Onagh Bridge, from near Crone Wood.

15. Glenasmole–Seefin Circuit

*Glencree – Glassamucky Brakes – Glenasmole – Black Hill –
Seefin – Kippure – Sally Gap – Glencree*

Location: Wicklow

Distance: 38km

Duration: 2.5 to 3 hours

Grade: 3

Height Gain: 804m

Verdict: A super, rare and unusual route through hidden Kippure.

The turn at Castlekelly Bridge, close to Glenasmole Reservoir.

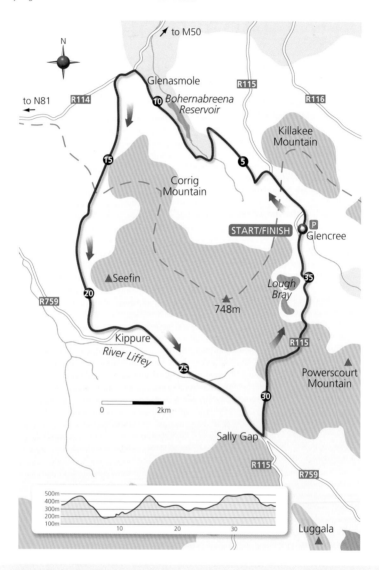

Start/finish

Glencree visitor centre in north County Wicklow. There is ample parking within the grounds of the centre, best accessed by car coming from the Rathfarnham/Dundrum direction, taking the R115 towards Killakee, and

Glencree and the Old Oak Valley at the height of summer.

following the Military Road into Glencree. At the junction at the top of Glencree Valley, take the sharp left, and the Glencree visitor will be just a few hundred metres along on the right.

'Cycling is a living, breathing art,' wrote Laurent Fignon in his autobiography, *We Were Young and Carefree* (originally published in French, in 2009, as *Nous étions jeunes et insouciants*). Sporting books don't come much more philosophical than this; poignant too, not just because Fignon is best remembered as the man who lost the closest ever Tour de France finish (in 1989, by eight seconds, to the American Greg LeMond) as opposed to the man who won it twice (in 1983 and 1984), and also because he died of cancer, in 2010, aged only 50.

'And that is the magic of cycling,' he wrote, 'the simple forward motion from the power in your legs treats you to great bursts of freedom. Your legs and nothing more. That's the little miracle that is the bike, where man and machine conjoin. It's a unique invention. The fusion of a man with himself.'

Cycling, perhaps more than any other sport, lends itself to the written word. One of the original and best is *The Rider* by Tim Krabbé, which, like *On the Road* and *The Great Gatsby*, is best read in a slow and continuous loop. To the last word it's the perfect paean to all the pain and pleasure and the fellowship of the road bike. From the opening paragraph, where Krabbé looks at the non-riders around him – 'the emptiness of those lives shocks me' – it is, by turns of the page, subjectively arrogant and despairingly real. It was written in 1978 and reads even louder today.

> The greater the suffering, the greater the pleasure. That is nature's payback to riders for the homage they pay her by suffering. Velvet pillows, safari parks, sunglasses; people have become woolly mice. Instead of expressing their gratitude for the rain by getting wet, people walk around with umbrellas. Nature is an old lady with few friends these days, and those who wish to make use of her charms, she rewards passionately.

This route has become one of my favourites in Wicklow for those reasons, offering a fair dose of suffering and pleasure, but with passionate expressions of nature throughout.

The starting point – or rendezvous point, if you prefer – is the Glencree visitor centre: I'd normally come at this route from the Glencree Valley, coming up from Enniskerry, but for the purpose of this guide, the start and finish is at the visitor centre.

From the Glencree visitor centre turn left, then continue for a short while where the L1011 meets the Military Road (R115). Here, turn sharp right onto the Military Road, back in the direction of Dublin city. It's a bit of a climb out of Glencree and then up and across the Featherbeds, especially if the wind is blowing.

Just after the Wicklow/Dublin border, marked by the sudden change in road surface from rougher to smoother, turn left down onto the R7236, and down towards the Glenasmole Reservoir. This descent, again while great fun, requires some caution as the road is narrow, and yes, slippery when wet.

The road bends, then continues straight. Veer left at the gentle fork in the road, down into the townland of Glassamucky Brakes. At the junction at the bottom of the hill, turn left and continue on past the scattering of stone cottages that make up Glenasmole until reaching the Castlekelly Bridge.

This crosses over the River Dodder not long before the river spills into the reservoir. After the bridge, turn sharp right. From here, the road soon runs parallel to the first of the two reservoirs. The road then dips gently before climbing again, running alongside the reservoirs down to the right, with Ballymorefinn Hill to the left, this stretch of road sheltered by a healthy cluster of large Scots pine.

Continuing mostly straight, the road then drops again and meets the stop sign at the junction with the main R114. Turn onto this road, at the townland of Ballinascorny Lower, and continue for a few hundred metres, then take the left turn off the road, heading up the side of Black Hill, to the right.

It's a stiff climb for the next few kilometres, yet beautifully peaceful. To the right are sweeping views over west County Dublin, and in summer the fields below appear like rivers of ferns. The road continues mostly straight and passes through the Dublin/Wicklow border, at about 16.5km, and continues until it reaches the entrance to the Kilbride Rifle Range.

The road then dips slightly down the side of Seefin, off to the left of the road. The peak itself, which is marked by a Neolithic passage tomb, can't be seen from the road, but is certainly worth a visit another day by foot. It dates back approximately 5,000 years and appears to be part of a series of tombs, as the nearby peaks of Seefingan and Seahan also have similar cairns covering old passage tombs. Seefin was not fully excavated until 1931, although no artefacts were discovered nor, indeed, any traces of human remains.

The road then sweeps around the left, along the edge of the forest, through what must be one of the most peaceful stretches of road in Wicklow. The traffic is invariably quiet because the road has no major commuting purpose, unlike some of the other 'quiet' roads of Wicklow.

The route then emerges onto the R759, just before the entrance to Kippure Estate, and over the Kippure Bridge, under which runs Athdown Brook, one of the many tributaries of the River Liffey in the area.

Stay left for the long, slow but beautifully rewarding climb up the side of Kippure, to the left, and the Coronation Plantation to the right. About halfway up the climb the road briefly turns as it crosses over the River Liffey, then continues more or less straight until the reaching the Sally Gap.

At the crossroads, turn right, where the road very briefly rises but then mostly descends gently back down past the entrance to the RTÉ mast at Kippure, and from there down the side of Upper and Lower Lough Bray and finally back into Glencree, taking the right turn off the Military Road which leads back to the Glencree visitor centre.

The descent from the Sally Gap at Upper Lough Bray.

16. Rathdrum–Avoca Circuit

Rathdrum – Avondale – Meeting of the Waters – Avoca –
Woodenbridge – Aughrim – Ballinaclash – Rathdrum

Location: Wicklow

Distance: 34km

Duration: 2.5 to 3 hours

Grade: 3

Height Gain: 406m

Verdict: Gently undulating ride through some of Wicklow's most scenic towns and villages.

Monument to Charles Stewart Parnell at Rathdrum.

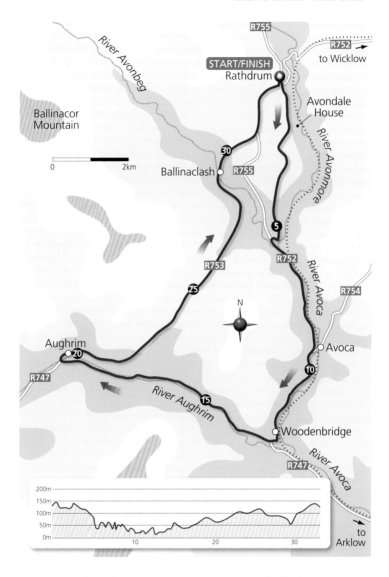

Start/finish

Rathdrum in south County Wicklow. There is ample parking in and around the village. The main access route by car is off the M11: take the exit at Rathnew and follow the signposts and R752 into Rathdrum.

The entrance to Avondale House and Woodland Park.

No Irish politician has a stronger association with County Wicklow than Charles Stewart Parnell, one of the great leaders and liberators of his time, which justifiably earned him the title of 'Uncrowned King of Ireland'.

This route starts out as a little homage to Parnell, passing his birthplace at Avondale House, the centrepiece of the majestic Avondale Forest Park. The entire 500-acre estate is now open to the public and includes the Charles Stewart Parnell Museum, which demands a visit if time and scheduling allow (see http://visitwicklow.ie/attractions/avondale-house-forest-park for opening hours and entry fees).

Starting out from the town of Rathdrum, which on its eastern side also boasts the Parnell National Memorial Park, the route heads south-east out through the crossroads with the main R752, following the signposts and towards Avondale House.

It's a short and quiet stretch of road through Corballis Demesne where, after just 1.5km, the main entrance to Avondale is now facing you. Avondale House was built in 1777 for Samuel Hayes, a pioneer of the reforestation of Ireland, who planted many thousands of trees on the estate. He left it to his friend and fellow MP Sir John Parnell in 1795, Charles Stuart's great-grandfather.

This is where Parnell was born in 1846. His political career began in earnest in 1874, when he became High Sheriff of Wicklow, his focus then drawn to the Home Rule League, formed in 1873 to campaign for some degree of self-government, and that was to become the primary cause of his relatively short yet immeasurably important influence on the later establishment of the Irish Free State. He was also one of the most powerful figures in the British House of Commons in the 1880s, before he died in 1891, aged just 45. After Parnell's death, the estate was sold to a Dublin butcher, who felled most of the trees to recoup his investment. Most of the woodlands were later renewed in 1904, when the estate was sold to the government, who developed it as a forestry school.

The route veers right after passing the entrance to Avondale, then veers left again, following the quieter back road towards the Meeting of the Waters, down the west bank of the Avonmore River. It is an undulating road but about as peaceful as it gets.

At the next junction, turn right, then not long after take a left turn back onto the main R752, at Meetings Bridge – where the Avonmore and Avonbeg rivers merge into Avoca River. It's a beautiful spot and inspired Thomas Moore to pen his famous Irish melody, 'The Meeting of the Waters'.

There is not in this wide world a valley so sweet
As that vale in whose bosom the bright waters meet!
Oh the last rays of feeling and life must depart
Ere the bloom of that valley shall fade from my heart.

The route then continues down the R752 and through the Vale of Avoca until it reaches the village of Avoca, charmingly nestled on the banks of

The bridge over the Avonbeg River at Ballinaclash.

the Avoca River. The original home of Avoca Handweavers, the village also earned some fame as the location for the BBC series *Ballykissangel*, featuring a young Colin Farrell, amongst others.

The main part of the village is over the bridge, on the left, and a perfect stop-off point, even at this early stage. The route then continues along the R752 past some of the old Avoca copper mines and down into the sleepy village of Woodenbridge.

The Woodenbridge Hotel and Lodge, established in 1608, claims to be one of the oldest hotels in Ireland, and certainly is a haven of peace and tranquillity. Here, the R757 meets the R747, and we turn right, following the signpost for Aughrim. This is another sweet stretch of road, albeit quite narrow and winding in places, as it follows the Aughrim River for about 7km into the village.

Aughrim is entered by turning right, over the bridge across the river, and then right again, heading out on the R753 back towards Ballinaclash. Aughrim has been repeatedly named Wicklow's Tidiest Village, and for good reason. It is also the site of Wicklow GAA's home pitch, better known as 'fortress Aughrim'. The Rednagh Bridge, a little further south of the village where the Ow and Derry rivers meet to form the Aughrim River, was the site of a famous confrontation during the 1798 Rebellion.

There is a slight climb on the road back to Ballinaclash, with Cushbawn Mountain off to the left. The road passes through Crone Beg and Crone More and what is known as 'the Straight Mile', before turning slightly left again into the hamlet of Ballinaclash, which, like most villages on this route, is also situated on a bridge, over the Avonbeg.

From here the route follows the R753 for a short while, with a bit of an incline, before it reaches the R755 again, and continues left back towards Rathdrum. The road veers right, the route then finishing with a left turn back into Rathdrum.

17. Little Sugar Loaf to the Sea

Kilmacanogue – Little Sugar Loaf – Greystones – Kilcoole – Newcastle – Rathnew – Glenealy – Moneystown – Annamoe – Roundwood – Kilmacanogue

Location: Wicklow

Distance: 67km

Duration: 3 to 3.5 hours

Grade: 4

Height Gain: 670m

Verdict: Beautifully rewarding ride from the mountains to the sea and back.

Wicklow coastline near Newcastle.

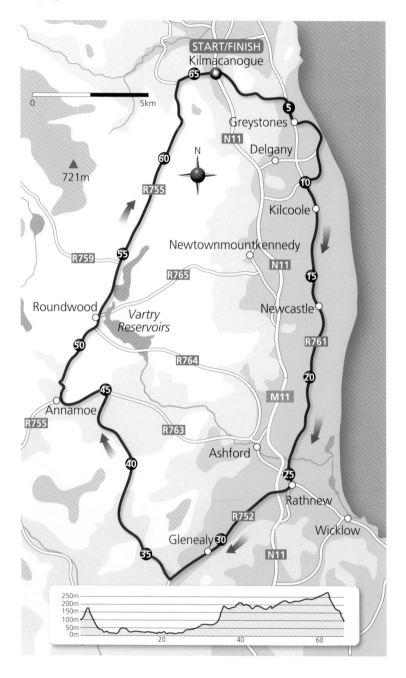

Start/finish

Kilmacanogue in north County Wicklow, which has a few parking options on some of the surrounding slip roads. Head south on the M50/M11/N11 and take the Kilmacanogue exit, not long after the Bray exit on the left.

Wicklow mountain gorse in bloom in early summer.

Anyone who has taken the ferry from either England or France and sailed into Dublin Bay will tell you one of the first things that truly mark your arrival is the backdrop of the Dublin Mountains, whose proximity to the sea is certainly stark, and in turn parts of the Wicklow Mountains; and the view back out to sea is returned from many vantage points within and atop those same mountains.

This route is mostly about combining the two views – of the Dublin mountains and the Irish Sea, setting off from the foothills of the Wicklow Mountains and then heading out along the sea. It affords fine views of the sea, firstly, and from there back towards the mountains, before finishing back at the starting point.

From Kilmacanogue, the route goes out over the N11, which means heading for the small roundabout, turning left (i.e. taking the first exit) and going across the flyover. At the next roundabout just over the flyover, take the first exit, left onto Bohilla Lane, which skirts up the side of the Little Sugar Loaf. It is a steep 2km climb, but the reward at the top of the hill is the first sweeping views out across the sea, and St George's Channel, with Bray Head off to the left and Greystones down to the right.

The route then passes along Templecarrig Upper and the top side of the Glen of the Downs golf course, on the right-hand side of the road, before descending swiftly to the junction with the R761: here turn right, following the road into Greystones, all the while with those wonderful sea views off to the left.

Follow the road into Greystones, which veers left onto Rathdown Road, then take a right turn onto Church Road and through the town itself. Originally a small fishing village, Greystones was named after the 1km stretch of grey stones between two beaches on the seafront. The town has grown significantly in recent years, yet retains its welcoming charm,

Trees lining the route along Roundwood reservoir in Wicklow

with a wide selection of cafés and ice-cream shops and the now-famous vegetarian restaurant, The Happy Pear.

Continue out of Greystones as the road veers around right after the DART station onto Mill Road, and at the first roundabout, take the first exit and head out past Greystones Rugby Club. Continue through the next five small roundabouts, then at the Charlesisland roundabout, take the first exit and the road signposted Kilcoole.

It is a short, flat 2km stretch into Kilcoole, one of Wicklow's best-known seaside villages, not least as the set for the Irish TV series *Glenroe*, which ran through the 1980s and 1990s and was something a household staple each Sunday evening. Irish-American writer J.P. Donleavy wrote his debut novel *The Ginger Man* while living in the village.

Continue straight through, staying on the R761. The road soon passes the back of Druids Glen Golf Club, on the right-hand side of the road, and the entrance to the Kilcoole Golf Club on the left.

The village of Newcastle is then passed on the left, named, naturally enough, after the Norman castle that once occupied the spot. It has long since disappeared, destroyed in the 16th century. The current ruin is of a fortified building that was later erected on the site.

From here it is another straight run down into Rathnew, with frequent views of the sea still off to the left, and occasionally the view extends ever further south towards Wicklow town. Before reaching Rathnew, the road meets the R772, where we turn left into the town itself.

Head briefly up Main Street before taking a right turn, onto the R752, signposted Glenealy. The road passes under the M11 motorway and continues for just under 5km before reaching Glenealy, which despite some rapid expansion in recent years remains a little oasis of sorts, marked on all sides by fields and forests.

Continue straight for another 2km until the road reaches Deputy's Pass, a nature reserve area passed on the left, and here turn right, onto the L2116, which now winds through a small forested valley, with Carrick Mountain to the north and Ballinastraw to the south-west. Continue to Garyduff Cross Roads, then turn right up towards Moneystown, another pleasantly scenic and largely unspoiled stretch of road.

After passing Moneystown National School on the right, the road continues to wind up to the Moneystown Bridge, where the route turns right and up to the Tomriland Cross Roads, and the junction with the R763. Turn left, and follow the road down towards Annamoe, the majestic Castlekevin dominating the landscape to the right, once the site of a large medieval fortress. Later, John Millington Synge spent many a summer of his youth in the old country house that now stands on the east side of Castlekevin.

The road then drops to the junction with the R755, Annamoe just off to the left, as this route turns right towards Roundwood. This stretch of road was recently resurfaced and is pleasant to ride on, although it can be busy, especially at weekends.

It's a steady enough climb for the 5km or so into Roundwood. There are plenty of pubs in the village worthy of a brief rest, not least the Roundwood Inn, and from here it's a straight run up the R755 back towards Kilmacanogue. The Great Sugar Loaf soon comes into view to the right, before the road drops sharply for a wonderfully thrilling descent back into Kilmacanogue and the starting point.

18. Aghavannagh through Tinahely Loop

Drumgoff – Aghavannagh – Knockananna – Tinahely –
Ballinglen – Aughrim – River Ow – Aghavannagh – Drumgoff

Location: Wicklow

Distance: 60km

Duration: 2.5 to 3 hours

Grade: 4

Height Gain: 1,199m

Verdict: Majestic rolling loop deep in hidden Wicklow.

The bridge approaching Drumgoff Inn at Glenmalure.

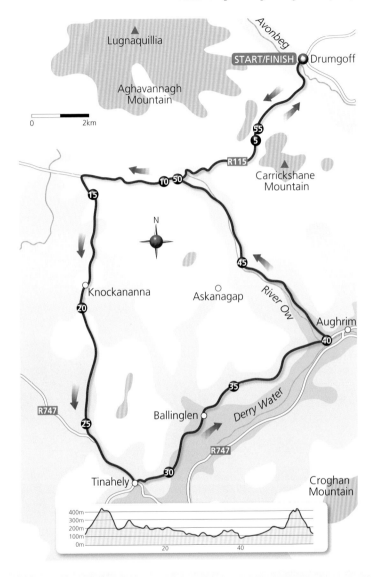

Start/finish

Drumgoff in south County Wicklow, which has good parking space for visitors. The main access route by car is off the M11, taking the exit at Rathnew and following the signpost and R752 into Rathdrum, and from there following the signpost for Drumgoff/Glenmalure.

N ot long into *The Rider*, that enduring classic of cycling fiction by Tim Krabbé, there is a little anecdote that neatly captures the professional cyclist's utter obsession with weight. In some ways it makes sense and in other ways it makes no sense at all. Jacques Anquetil, the five-time winner of the Tour de France, used to take his water bottle out of its bike cage before every climb and stick it in the back pocket of his jersey. Ab Geldermans, his Dutch lieutenant, watched him do this for years, until finally he couldn't stand it any more and asked why. Anquetil, in typical debonair French, explained: a rider is made up of two parts – the person and the bike. The bike, of course, is the instrument the person uses to go faster, but its weight also slows him down on the steepest inclines. His secret was to ensure the bike was as light as possible. One quick and simple way of doing this was to take the water bottle out its bike cage, transferring the weight to the rider. Makes sense?

What is certain is that riding up a hill on a bicycle, either professionally or purely recreationally, is a lot easier when carrying a lighter load, as in lighter body weight. Style can help too, however, and since switching largely from running to cycling, I have found that similar 'rules' of style appear to apply – especially when riding up hills. My first rule of running style is to remember to 'run with the legs, not on them', subconsciously

Passing over the Ow River.

The 1798 monument at Aughrim.

shifting your weight to your upper body. And this seems to work just as well in cycling: riding with the legs, not on them. Also, when running, it's best to keep the hips held forward, engaging the core stomach muscles, and this style also works well while cycling, especially when out of the saddle and standing on the pedals.

This route may not be the most demanding in this guidebook, although it does climb over the side of Slieve Maan on the way out of Drumgoff, and again on the way back. The rest of it makes for near-perfect cycling style and rhythm, especially on the beautifully serene route out of Aughrim and up along the banks of the River Ow and back into Aghavannagh. Again, this may not be the so-called fashionable side of Wicklow, but it is every bit as scenic, with its tree-clad valleys and fast-flowing rocky streams.

Starting out from Drumgoff, the route heads south-west on the Military Road, in the direction of Aghavannagh. After crossing the River Avonbeg, you can see the remnants of Drumgoff Barracks to the left, which, unlike the other barracks built in tandem with the Military Road, was never fully occupied. According to reports of the time, on the first attempt to set up camp there, soldiers were ambushed by the rebels and retreated to Rathdrum. Before their next attempt, it went on fire and then fell into disuse.

After the climb around the side of Slieve Maan, cycle over the Aghavannagh Bridge and the River Ow and more or less straight to

Mullin Cross Roads, at about 14km, where the route turns left, signposted Knockananna.

Passing through Kilcarney Crossroads, it's a mostly flat stretch into the small village of Knockananna, which translates from the Irish, *Cnoc an Eanaigh*, as 'hill of the marsh'. Continue straight through the village on the road signposted Tinahely, the last road in west Wicklow before the Kildare border.

At about 26km, the road merges onto the R747, just after passing over the Derry River, and from there continue left down along the banks of the river and into Tinahely, also passing one of the last crossing points of the Wicklow Way.

Tinahely's old market origins are evident by the layout of the village, although what makes it unusual is that there is no parish church; instead, St Kevin's church is located some 2km east of the village in the townland of Kilaveny. The Derry River is one of the many tributaries of the River Slaney, and runs off to the south of the village. The Courthouse Arts Centre in Tinahely regularly hosts art and cultural events.

This route then turns off east, taking a left turn on entering Tinahely, and following the road out toward Ballinglen, which essentially runs parallel to the R747 back into Aughrim, but a far more peaceful and enjoyable ride. Continue straight through Ballinglen where the road now climbs a little, before reaching the Roddenagh Bridge.

Turn left here, with Auhgrim village itself straight ahead, and so begins a magnificent ride up along the valley of the River Ow and back towards Aghavannagh. It is a beautifully sheltered valley and passes through some dense forestry, and also the tiny hamlet of Ballymanus, birthplace of Billy Byrne, one of the heroes of the 1798 Rebellion.

Off to the right-hand side of the road is Coolballintaggart, some 536m high, while to the west is Coolgarrow. The main forest entrance is then passed on the right, before the road passes over the Ballygobben Bridge and back to the junction with the Military Road. Turn right here, and back up over the side of Slieve Maan, all the while remembering to be riding with the legs, not on them.

19. Baltinglass– Hollywood Circuit

Baltinglass – Hollywood – Wicklow Gap – Laragh – Drumgoff – Aghavannagh – Rathdangan – Baltinglass

Location: Wicklow

Distance: 84km

Duration: 3.5 to 4 hours

Grade: 4

Height Gain: 1,399m

Verdict: Beautifully sweeping ride from Baltinglass, then over the Wicklow Gap in reverse.

The junction at Hollywood village, turning left and towards the Wicklow Gap.

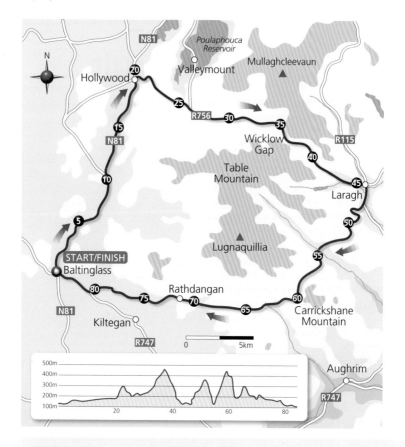

Start/finish

Baltinglass in west County Wicklow. There is plenty of parking space in and around the village. The main access route by car is the N81, or by taking the R747 from the M9.

There are six steel screws and a five-inch titanium bar where my left collarbone used to be. There's a tiny piece of bone floating beneath my left kneecap, and a bite-like scar down the back of my right calf muscle.

'Don't freak out,' the nurse told me, 'but that's about the worst collarbone break we've ever seen.'

And that was 24 hours later. Because after that seemingly harmless crash on the Enniskerry Road, a few years back, I'd got back on my bike, cycled home, then gone to bed with a bag of ice strapped across my

View down to Glendasan Valley from the Wicklow Gap.

shoulder. Only the next day when the swelling turned purple and then a horrible black were my worst fears realised: I'd need an operation to get that collarbone fixed.

And I go cycling for the sheer pleasure of it! It's all part of the spirit of the sport: ride on, don't look back, deal with the consequences later. 'Put me back on my bike,' cried Tom Simpson, after collapsing in the 1967 Tour de France, just 1.5km from the summit of Mont Ventoux. Simpson had pushed himself to the point of oblivion, although what the roadside medics didn't realise was that he'd also consumed several shots of amphetamines and brandy before the climb – a fatal combination, as it turned out, as he was pronounced dead on arrival to hospital.

Mont Ventoux, at 1,912m the highest and loneliest peak in Provençal France, is also nicknamed the 'Beast of Provence', and for good reason. True cycling enthusiasts will say that you haven't properly conquered it unless you've ridden up its three routes: south from Bédoin, north-west from Malaucène, and east from Sault.

The Wicklow Gap, which by road reaches a peak at around 477m, is certainly no Mont Ventoux, but that doesn't mean it doesn't deserve to be conquered from both sides – which is where this route comes in: Routes 6 and 9 both feature sections of the Wicklow Gap going east–west, whereas this route crosses it west–east, which is an entirely different experience, taking in parts of the somewhat less-fashionable west Wicklow. With five notable climbs, it's also one of the toughest routes of this guide.

The starting point is the village of Baltinglass, close to the border with both Carlow and Kildare, on the banks of the River Slaney. It has an ancient past typical of the area and the original Irish name, 'the way of Conglas', refers to Conglas of the mythological warrior collective, the Fianna.

At the north end of the village on the weir of the River Slaney is the ruin of Baltinglass Abbey, which had many additions over the centuries, and is believed to date back to 700 AD.

The route goes out this way, heading along the N81, following the River Slaney, which frequently comes into view from both sides of the road. It's just under 20km along this road, heading towards Hollywood, and while mostly flat, there are some sweeping turns, as it passes the road to Stratford, to the left, passes over the River Carrigower, and along the side of Hollywood Glen.

The right turn to Hollywood is not particularly well signposted and is best recognised by the petrol station, which is on the left-hand side after you make the turn onto what is now the R756. Stay right as the road heads into Hollywood, bypassing most of the village, which is off to the left. The road then passes the old Church of Ireland church, with several sites associated with St Kevin to the left. Look out for the Hollywood sign, perched on the hill to the right.

The village has been used for many 'Hollywood' productions, including Neil Jordan's *Michael Collins*, some scenes of which were shot here; the ambush and shooting of Collins at Béal na Bláth were filmed in Corrigan's Glen just outside the village itself.

The road climbs up the side of Slievecorragh and then levels out for a while, crossing over the King's River at about 25.5km. Then begins the long, slow climb up towards the Wicklow Gap, gradual at first, but kicking up at about 30km as the road crosses between Fair Mountain, to the right, and the back of the bulking Tonelagee.

The reward, however, is the wonderfully curving descent all the way down towards Glendalough, past two viewing points on the right, and the turn-off to the Turlough Hill Reservoir. At the bottom of the hill the road levels out and then reaches a yield sign. This is the R757, the right turn heading back into Glendalough; stay left, however, and continue into Laragh, and then take the right turn at the top of the village, signposted Rathdrum, and onto the R755.

Drumgoff Inn at Glenmalure.

The route then turns right and joins up with the Military Road, up the side of Derrybawn, signposted Glenmalure/L2083/Aghavannagh. It's a tough ascent, passing the Shay Elliott Memorial, the same stretch of climb covered in Route 7.

After the descent to the Glenmalure valley floor, at Drumgoff, continue straight, crossing over the Avonbeg River, in the direction of Aghavannagh.

So begins another climb, up the side of Slieve Maan, again in the opposite direction as the one covered in Route 9, and again an entirely different experience. It's a wonderfully scenic ride at any time of the year. The road then drops down over the Aghavannagh Bridge, before the last gentle climb, skirting the edges of Slieveboy Mountain off to the right.

It is a straight ride into Rathdangan. Go through the crossroads here, continuing on up to Graigue, where the road continues straight through another crossroads, before joining the R747 at Woodfield. From here, on the last few kilometres into Baltinglass, the route passes the industrial estate on the right, then goes through Weaver's Square in the village, and finally back over the River Slaney on Main Street to the starting point.

20. 1998 Tour de France in Ireland Stage

*O'Connell Street – Dundrum – Shankill – Bray – Kilmacanogue –
Ashford – Rathnew – Wicklow – Arklow – Avoca – Woodenbridge
– Rathdrum – Laragh – Wicklow Gap – Hollywood – Blessington –
Tallaght – Kilmainham – Phoenix Park*

Location: Dublin/Wicklow	**Grade:** 5
Distance: 185km	**Height Gain:** 1,794m
Duration: 6 to 7 hours	**Verdict:** That rare chance to ride a stage of the Tour de France – in Ireland!

Coming under the Luas bridge at Dundrum, with the Dublin Mountains coming into full view.

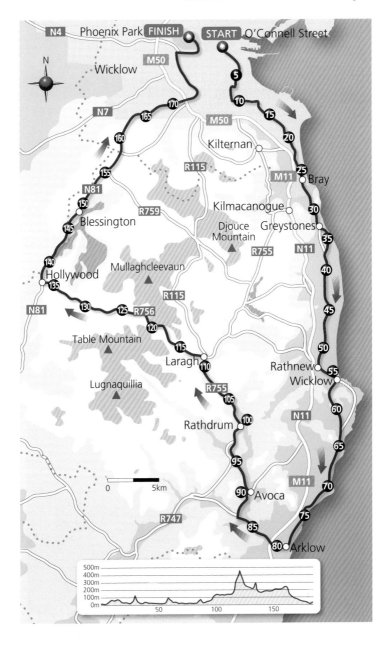

Start/finish

O'Connell Street, Dublin city centre, where on-street parking is usually at a premium. If arriving by car, the best option would be to park at the finish, at the Phoenix Park, where there is ample parking, always free, and cycle the short distance up the River Liffey to connect with the official 1998 Tour de France starting point.

There is something gently ironic about the idea that the first and possibly last time the Tour de France started in this country, it ended up showing off not the beauty of the Irish countryside, including parts of Wicklow, but rather the ugly side of cycling. Because the 1998 Tour, more than any before or since, will always be best remembered for the full and shocking exposure of cycling's doping problem. It had been happening for years before and quite a few years after, and no sport will ever be entirely rid of doping, but it seemed no one was quite prepared for, nor, indeed, suspected the full extent to which it was going on, as the aftermath of this Tour revealed in all its gory detail, beginning with what became known as the Festina affair.

It just so happened that around the same as the teams and riders were being introduced in Dublin Castle on the eve of the race, Friday 10 July, Willy Voet, the Festina team *soigneur*, or masseur, was stopped by police at the Franco-Belgian border, on his way to Dublin for the start of the race. His car was checked and in two cooler bags behind his seat the police found 234 doses of the blood-booster EPO, 80 flasks of human growth hormone, 160 capsules of testosterone and 60 pills of Asaflow, a sort of highly potent aspirin.

Cycling up the Wicklow Gap, the same route as Stage 2 of the 1998 Tour de France in Ireland.

Riders in the Wicklow 200 cycle event begin the ascent of the Wicklow Gap.

In his terrifying confessional *Breaking the Chain* published a few years later, Voet claimed this sort of doping abuse was rampant in the peloton, certainly not just within Festina, and that the chances of being caught for taking such banned substances were somewhere around zero.

The Tour started as normal, although by the end of Saturday's prologue time trial in Dublin, all the talk was of doping. Sunday's first stage proper, 12 July, was primarily about showing off parts of the Wicklow Mountains, including the Wicklow Gap, but already it felt like the entire race was under a dark cloud of suspicion, which of course it was. Which is a shame, because a lot of work had gone into preparing the route and the roads, and a lot of people came out to support it on the day. That dirty doping controversy aside, the 1998 Tour also has some personal significance and affection in that provided one of my first 'breaks' in sports journalism. That summer, fresh out of finishing an MA at Dublin City University, I was on a two-month work placement at *The Irish Times*, and had yet to produce anything that might be considered worthy – or, indeed, wordy. Partly by chance, partly by desperation, I suggested to a friend, Aidan Brosnan, that we cycle the two Tour de France stages in Ireland in advance of the race as a sort of test run – the Dublin–Wicklow stage, followed by the Enniscorthy–Cork stage, which was set for the Monday. As ill-prepared as we both were, he agreed. I wrote up the articles the week of the race, and convinced the Sports Editor to extend the placement into something more permanent.

On that note, the Tour stage into Wicklow is certainly worthy revisiting, and so here it is.

The route in 1998 covered 180.5km, starting from O'Connell Street, then heading out via College Green, Nassau Street, Ballsbridge and Milltown Road to Dundrum, where the race had its 'official start' at the Stephen Roche Monument on the main Dundrum Road.

From here the stage proceeded through Stillorgan, Shankill, Bray, Kilmacanogue, Ashford, through Rathnew and on to Wicklow town, where it turned onto the N11 at the Beehive. Given that much of the N11 is now motorway, it is not possible (or legal) to cycle the exact same route, so part of this stretch sticks to the old coast road, essentially all the way from Stillorgan and Shankill, into Bray on down to Rathnew, before rejoining the original Tour route at Arklow. It sticks to the original route as far Stillorgan, but instead of the motorway this route follows the cycle paths that line much of the old N11 at Cornelscourt, Cabinteely, and then into Shankill. Then stay on the old coast road all the way down through Bray, Greystones, Kilcoole Newcastle, Rathnew and Wicklow Town.

The route then heads inland to Avoca, Woodenbridge, Rathdrum, Laragh and then over the Wicklow Gap.

From there the route heads to Hollywood, back to Blessington, down the embankment to Tallaght, into Inchicore, past the historic Kilmainham Gaol and on into the Phoenix Park. In 1998, the race included a 7km circuit of the Phoenix Park before finishing on the main road opposite Arás an Uachtaráin. The stage was won in a bunch sprint by Belgium's Tom Steels, timed to finish at about 4 p.m. that afternoon, to avoid clashing with the 1998 World Cup final, which took place in Paris that evening.

Given the few minor detours necessitated by avoiding the motorway, this route comes in at about 185km, and is actually largely flat, with the obvious exception of the Wicklow Gap. If only for posterity's sake, here is how I described the ride that July of 1998.

'On the trail of the Tour',
The Irish Times, Tuesday, 7 July 1998

All this talk of road closures, sporting spectacles and the grand scale of things got me thinking. Just where is this *Tour de France* en Irlande going and do these cyclists really deserve such fussing over?

I decided on some method journalism to find out exactly what the riders have in front of them. Packing a map and some essential supplies, I recruited a companion and set out first thing on Sunday morning to cycle stage one of the 1998 Tour de France.

Of course, this was no race so I'd take my time. Besides, the only regular cycling I do is into town and back and my bike is not exactly a tour de force on the road.

The route looked pleasant enough. Cruise on down to Arklow and then back up through the scenic Wicklow Gap. A straight run into the Phoenix Park for the finish, about 180 km in all. It was supposed the take the riders a little over four hours, so even if I had to walk a bit, it could be easily done in a day.

Le Grand Depart. 9.00 a.m.
Plenty of strong coffee to kick off and then down to the Stephen Roche Monument in Dundrum for the official start. Not many people around at this hour and the village looks great with the huge array of flags and bunting. Photo-opportunity number one over and it's off into the unknown.

The monument to Stephen Roche, winner of the 1987 Tour de France, at Dundrum village.

A sharp left-hand turn out of Dundrum village leads up the steep Kilmacud Road. It's breathtaking already, although not the type associated with excitement. Thanks to the adrenalin, the road up from Stillorgan to Shankill and Bray is easy. The main road in Bray is about the last scheduled to be resurfaced and threatens a puncture at this early stage. Still, Bray looks good and especially the decorations outside Duff's pub.

In less than an hour I'm on the N11 and heading straight for Wicklow. The road is quiet and the sun is shining, making the Glen of the Downs look every ounce worthy of the efforts of those eco-warriors. I don't know if it's the wind at my back or what, but I seem to be flying, racing almost. How much faster could the Tour be travelling? Bring on l'Alpe d'Huez!

No need to stop at either Ashford or Rathnew. A group of club cyclists appear to be gaining from behind, but they soon turn off left, obviously fearful of the Tour route. Bunch of amateurs.

Wicklow Town: Le Preview 1hr 40 mins, Le Tour 1 hr

It's straight through the town to admire all the colourful decorations. Unfortunately, I miss the turn to get back on the N11 and end up on the golf course road. Twenty navigational minutes later, it's past the Beehive (pub) and due south to Arklow.

Jack White's advertises special Tour de France lunches on race day, but Arklow beckons and the Lucozade will do for the moment. About 10 minutes later the hunger does set in and by the time I roll over the Arklow bridge, the legs are under local anaesthetic. It's time for lunch.

It's almost 1.00 p.m. leaving Arklow on the road for Woodenbridge. This is the first taste of the back roads and it's becoming a deeper green and emitting a stronger perfume with every pedal – the fragrance of the Garden of Ireland. The sweet valley is spoiled only by the noise and sight of Irish Fertilisers – an eyesore if ever there was one. Another rolling river into Woodenbridge and you're close to the heart of beauty personified. There's so much oxygen in the air down here that it could be on the banned substance list.

Avoca: Le Preview 4 hrs 30 mins, Le Tour 1 hr 35

Maybe I've been enjoying the view too much, because time is getting on. Then a wrong turn at Avoca becomes the first self-inflicted detour of the Tour route. Two direction inquiries – a local farmer and foreign caravan driver – proved useless and after a couple of miles in the wrong direction, I finally get back on track.

It's still an inspiring route through to Rathdrum and past the now customary 'This Road Will Be Closed' reminders of what will be coming here next week. I don't think I've even mentioned the quality of the roads so far. It's a cycling paradise and I'm happy that I won't be needing that puncture repair kit after all.

Rathdrum arrives and the first serious dose of tiredness sets in. It's a roller-coaster road into Laragh but the energy is low and I decide on my own feed station. The Tour riders munch on high-energy bars along the way but I settle for the more commercial type.

Laragh: Le Preview 6 hrs 20 mins, Le Tour 2 hrs 20

I fill the water bottle and head for the Col de Wicklow. There are some nasty clouds ahead but after this it's all downhill so nothing is going to stop me now. It's a fair old climb, all right, but the surface is immaculate and helps keep the momentum going.

About halfway up and the legs are gone. All those Sunday drivers are watching and there's no way I am going to stop and walk in front of them. Someone has painted on the road 'Kelly and Roche and You'. That's cool – only I don't do this for a living.

I made the mistake of looking at Paul Kimmage's book *A Rough Ride* last night. It's a great read but left me with this image of a knackered cyclist injecting amphetamines as a final boost before a race finish. At this stage, it wouldn't have taken too much convincing for me to do the same.

About an hour later I make it over the Gap. It's wet, I'm cold and about ready to eat a horse. The next point on the map is Hollywood, but God knows how far away that is. The road reminds me of Australia – 500 miles to the next gas station.

Hollywood: Le Preview 8 hrs, Le Tour 2 hrs 53 mins
At last, a shop. I have a can of Coke drunk before I get to the counter and munch on chocolate Goldgrain for the next few miles. It's enough of a boost to get me through Blessington and back on the Dublin road.

Finally the city comes into view. More confusion in trying to get the right road and then, after 10 hours on the bike, I roll into the Phoenix Park. The Tour does an eight-kilometre loop of the park, but I have to cycle back to Dundrum. Besides, Stage Two is just around the corner.

L'Arrivée: Le Preview 10 hrs 5 mins, Le Tour 4 hrs 6 mins

Summertime gorse in bloom on the descent from the Dublin Featherbeds down to Glenasmole Reservoir.